The Cycling ANTHOLOGY

VOLUME SIX

Edited by
Ellis Bacon
&
Lionel Birnie

PELOTON PUBLISHING
www.cyclinganthology.com

First published in Great Britain in 2015
by Peloton Publishing

Typeset by Peloton Publishing
Printed and bound by SS Media

ISBN 978-0-9932899-1-0
Jacket illustration by Simon Scarsbrook

Peloton Publishing Ltd
2 Gaddesden Lane, Redbourn, St Albans, AL3 7NP
Registered company number: 7353619

www.cyclinganthology.com
www.pelotonpublishing.co.uk
info@lionelbirnie.com

THE CYCLING ANTHOLOGY

THE CYCLING ANTHOLOGY

THE NEUTRALISED ZONE

INTRODUCTION BY THE EDITORS

So, here it is – volume six of *The Cycling Anthology*, which we hope you'll enjoy as much as the first five. If you're a new reader, welcome to a collection of cycling writing we like to think is like no other.

We know you won't have read any of these stories before; all of it is original writing, exclusive to *The Cycling Anthology*. But you may well recognise many of the writers' names from magazines, books, podcasts and television.

Returning for this volume are a number of writers from our stable, and we'd like to thank them for once again writing about the thoughts and themes close to their hearts. And welcome to the new ones, whose fantastic work appears for the first time.

We're lucky to have bestowed on us a rich and eclectic mix of subjects to fill these pages, and in this edition you'll be able to enjoy climbs and Classics, fact and fiction, history and Hemingway.

Thank you to all our readers and our contributors and see you here next time.

Ellis Bacon & Lionel Birnie

1

It might look – or sound – easy, but the life of a television cycling commentator is anything but.

Ned Boulting jumps out of the frying pan and into the burning depths of hell as he tries to get his head, and tongue, around a whole new way of speaking.

Can he talk the talk?

TELLING IT LIKE IT IS

BY NED BOULTING

It's like the first day of a new school year, marked by the same feeling of jittery anticipation and seasoned with good intentions. So I have everything laid out in front of me on my desk. I'm putting it in order. This is the easy bit.

The race is still two weeks away, but my work-space is a mess of stationery: Pritt Stick, scissors, pencils, Sharpies, highlighters and fine-writers, coloured card and see-through wallets. I am devilishly quick now with the routine, my left hand sometimes overtaking the right, as they complete separate functions; building, building the big picture all the while.

For days I have been phoning all my contacts on the teams heading to Yorkshire – prying, seeking out snippets of information, trying to get a steer. I've been making notes, trying to commit to memory as much as I can of 144 separate biographies. But time is beginning to run out, and soon the job will be done. After that, and rather terrifyingly, it's down to me.

I still don't know what I'll say when the red light goes on. I hope to hell I think of something good.

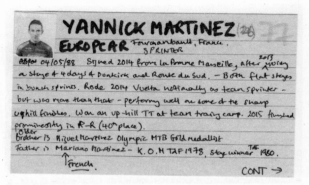

YANNICK MARTINEZ (28)
EUROPCAR Fouchambault, France.
SPRINTER
DOB 04/05/88 Signed 2014 from La Pomme Marseille, after winning 2013
a stage & 4 days & Donkirk and Route du Sud. — Both flat stages
in bunch sprints. Rode 2014 Vuelta nationally as team sprinter —
but was more than that — performing well on some of the sharp
uphill finishes. Won an up-hill TT at team training camp. 2015 finished
prominently in P-R (40th place).
older
Brother is Miguel Martinez Olympic MTB Gold medallist
Father is Mariano Martinez — K.O.H TdF 1978, Stage winner TdF 1980.
   French.
                                                    CONT →

My education in broadcasting took place in the highly-strung world of football. Given that the book you are reading quite clearly states its purpose on the front cover, with the word 'Cycling' rather prominent in that mission statement, I'll keep this digression brief. It is, however, relevant, since it goes to the heart of what it means to commentate, as opposed to report, or present. All these roles may appear to be interchangeable, but they are in fact substantively differentiated. I have reported and presented. But now, old dog that I am, I'm trying to learn a new trick.

The thing is, something's happened to me that has made me unrecognisable to myself.

I have crossed the Rubicon and signed up to membership of a very strange, very small band of people indeed. I have become a commentator.

Never for a minute did I think that one day

I would join their number. They were manifestly apart, I always felt; an odd breed, with pale fleshy hands and an indoor pallor. Sure, I counted a good few among my associates, from spells at Sky Sports and ITV Football, and could pass the time of day with most of them, over the breakfast table, or more likely at the check-in desk at Gatwick Airport en route to some minor sporting occasion. But, such was their sheer *otherness*, I would often try to curtail the conversation on some or other improvised pretext, breaking into their sporting stream of consciousness that passed for conversation.

They barely noticed that they were actually talking, rather than thinking. '… never quite recaptured their form since the cruciate knee injury…'

'Sorry to interrupt.' Then I would suddenly discover some hitherto unknown urge. 'I just need to get… one of those… things, from that shop… over there.'

'Oh, right you are. I'll crack on with my notes.' So, with a wry, put-upon smile that was nonetheless edged with smouldering glee, the television commentator would normally produce from his fearsome carry-on bag a colossal black folder, stuffed with minutely scribbled information. 'Got some catching up to do after the weekend's results.'

'Good. I'll leave you to it.'

I would take my leave, confident that I was not cut from the same cloth as the commentator (sheepskin, normally). The men in the padded coats may well have been one step short of actual madness, I believed, but they were already fully conversant with mania. They were overgrown boys with the imagination of Homer. They were the poets of the give and go, the high priests of the intelligent lay-off, the cantor of the strike on target:

'SHEAR-EERRRR!'

A nod and a breath. And then, as if in summary, an Amen…

'One-nil!'

Neurotic collection of information was, as far as I could tell, the defining hallmark of the commentator; the one thing they all had in common. They washed themselves in facts, pulled on pyjamas woven from analysis, brushed their teeth with anti-bacterial statistics and lay their fizzing heads on pillows stuffed with recent form. Unless they were fed and watered with information on an hourly basis, they would wilt and wither away.

I remember one hellishly early morning at Teesside Airport, waiting to board a chartered plane to Greece, on which I would be flying in the company of Middlesbrough Football Club to some underwhelming fixture in the group stages of the UEFA Cup. It can't have been much past five thirty in the morning, and I had my chin nuzzled sleepily into my chest, slumped into a plastic chair waiting to board.

Then my phone rang.

It was Jon Champion, ITV's commentator, who was flying out to the match from another airport.

'Ned, can you tell me if Stuart Parnaby is on the flight? I heard he might have picked up a knock in training.' (A 'knock' is commentary shorthand for an 'undefined injury'.)

'Sure, Jon. I'll try to find out.'

But who the hell was Stuart Parnaby? What on earth did he look like? I knew I should know, but I didn't know. I spent the next 20 minutes not walking up to Premier League footballers and not asking them if they were Stuart Parnaby. It was too humiliating. So I rang Jon back, and bluffed.

'No, Jon. He's not.'

'Ah. Good. Thought not.' Then he added, cryptically, 'Groin.'

I actively wished ill on the Parnaby groin. This faux information, however shabbily imparted, meant, presumably, that Jon could strike the unfortunate Parnaby from his list of possible picks for the team the following night. In one fell swoop, he had lightened his workload by some four per cent. (And in the end, thank God, it all turned out all right. Parnaby wasn't even on the bench.)

But I had learned a little of the particular neurosis of the commentator. I reeled in awe at the size of their task, the depth of their preparation, the diligence with which they approached it.

MERHAWI KUDUS (21)   86
MTN-QHUBEKA Asmara, Eritrea

23/01/94 - 58 kilos! Climber. Started racing + winny road race on
a MTB. Started out with Bretagne - Séché Environnement

2015 finished 7th on Stage 3 of Vuelta Andalucia (stage won by contador) ahead of Pete Kennagh,
Juergen von de Broeck, Sebastian Reichenbach.

2014 - 2nd GC Tour de Langkawi - 5th overall Route du Sud (climbing alongside
Rolla, Rogers and Valverde. Finished 2014 Vuelta, after heavy crash on
Stage One.
2013 2nd overall in Vuelta a Leon.

P. Robbie Hunter is his agent - he needs to gain a little muscle mp
t be a cavander

The football commentators I have worked with have
been among the most intelligent, talented, imagina-
tive voices I have ever listened to. But they are also,
in the public imagination, the most reviled, ludicrous,
unnecessary narcissists ever to slither their way into
the nation's living rooms. We surely can't both be
right. Maybe we are.

How you ever tried to watch a sporting event on
TV without the sound of a commentator's voice?
It's like trying to wash up without washing-up liquid.
The actions are all the same, but the effect is
nullified by silence and the distant background of
crowd hubbub.

Who knew that we needed the ramblings of a
middle-aged white man (let's face it, that's the de-
mographic) to imbue an occasion with a sense of
importance? It's only when they're not there that you
realise how much you miss them.

I remember taking one of my daughter's friends to a football match for the first time. They couldn't get accustomed to the lack of a voice. How were they supposed to interpret the event without someone intoning, 'Charlton now looking to get forward... but it's all too static... Jackson now, trying to pick out Kermorgant... and GIVES it AWAY... Leeds on the counter...' etc?

Yes, this is an uncomfortable truth: however much we think we don't, we do actually need our Motsons and our Walkers, our Colemans and O'Sullivans. Our Liggetts. Maybe we don't need Peter Alliss, but then again, maybe we don't need golf.

These voices all matter to us more than we care to admit. And yet, hating sports commentators from afar is a national sport at which we are considerably better than we are at the actual national sport itself.

During the 2006 World Cup, I came face to face with the effect this can have on the human beings in question.

Nine years ago, it must be remembered (and to think that such a time actually existed!), there was no Twitter. The internet was there, though, offering up a terrible temptation to the self-absorbed, or the less self-confident.

It was the day of a big match, a quarter-final, at an iconic stadium. About two hours before kick-off, I discovered one of ITV's distinguished and very experienced commentators sitting on the ground between two trucks, head bowed in gloom. When he noticed me, he looked up and declared with a trembling voice that he didn't feel he could go on air.

'If they don't want me, then what's the point? I'm just talking about the game I love. I don't intend to upset anyone.'

I fixed him a cup of tea and sat down next to him, trying to work out what the matter was. It seems that, during the preceding sleepless night, he'd Googled his own name and tripped over some vile abuse posted on some forum.

He couldn't clear these words from his mind. They had, overnight, come to define his weaknesses, at least in his eyes. He did go on to commentate on the game, and did so with trademark panache. But a bit of him was broken, and I vowed there and then never to seek out trouble in internet form.

Commentators are singled out because their input sits directly alongside the action. The presenters, the reporters, the pundits bookending the event in studios, just provide the padding around the game, but don't ever interrupt its flow. You can, and probably do, switch them off.

But the commentator is somehow intricately involved. That's his privilege and his curse.

I never intended to put my neck on the line. Yet here I am. Putting my neck on the line.

ANDY HAWDON (38) 174

RALEIGH-GAC

3/5/76

- Electrical engineer from Millom, Cumbria
- First pro contract
- Birthday on stage 3 (38)
- Sprinter - climbs ....
- Never ridden anything like this...
- Signed because they'd rather have him with them than against.
- Broke collarbone 5weeks ago in Belgium; bit a car bike 10 days ago
- Works at Sellafield.

When I moved from football into cycling, gradually shifting the weight of my job from the one booted foot to the other cleated one over the course of a decade, it was the voice of Phil Liggett (and his side-kick Paul Sherwen) that provided my soundtrack and my education.

'It's Roche! It's Stephen Roche!'

I don't mean his metaphorical voice, either. I mean his actual voice: the fleshy, stringy bit that vibrates in the larynx and slides through the frequencies as effortlessly as Tom Boonen over the cobbles. Liggett's voice is a rare thing, capable of both mellifluous rumination (with 75k still to run, the breakaway at 5'35" and the road bordered by sunflower fields) as well as rasping, breathless drama, when the sprint is in full cry and they're dropping like flies. And when the race gets high on mountain air and the decisive blows hang over the selection like invisible Damocles swords, he can change register again and impart grandeur to the action.

I marvelled at his ability to shift from humdrum to epic in the duration of one glottal stop, or hit the high notes from a standing start. I hope I am not giving away trade secrets when I reveal that, on occasion, the commentary is re-voiced for the highlights show. In the chaotic heat of a bunch sprint it is almost an inevitability that things will sometimes go awry. For heaven's sake, have you ever tried to call it in your heads? Lose your thread for just a fraction of a second and you'll find yourself instantly derailed, mouth open, simply watching the drama unfold. In a further second, it has happened without you and you've blown it.

So, from time to time, commentators are asked to pick up from the last 500 metres and re-commentate, with the glitches ironed out, but with all the same intensity and spontaneous excitement they had the first time around. Liggett would do this with consummate ease, jumping from nought to 60 in the space it took him to say, 'Cavendish!'

And now I had to follow this quality, match this experience? It seemed an absurd ambition. But in the winter of 2014, ITV decided that I should be tested. It seems I passed.

In the long months between being handed my commission and actually making my debut on the Tour de Yorkshire, I had plenty of time to graze the broadcasting landscape, picking up ideas, working out what I liked and what I liked less, and learning from others. There were many others to listen to, from the smooth experience of Simon Brotherton, through to the exemplary correctness of Eurosport's Rob Hatch, the excitable character of Carlton Kirby, and the insider wit of both Dan Lloyd and Matt Stephens. They all seemed marvellously self-assured, elegantly fluent.

All this watching telly only added to my anxiety. So I lost myself once again in stationery; cutting and sticking and scribbling notes. The detail would be my safety harness, I hoped. Thus the dormant 12-year-old in me awoke – the same callow youth who used to walk into travel agents and ask if they had an old copy of the previous year's International Flight Timetables Manual they could donate. I'd take the thousand-page book home and begin to copy out the information into notebooks. I still have a red exercise book into which I have diligently transcribed the domestic schedule for Olympic Airlines flights in 1982.

Preparation. Fail to prepare, prepare to fail. And all that guff.

Then the key question of a co-commentator arose. To my mind, and, thankfully, in the eyes of our producers too, the first and only name that sprang to mind was David Millar. Who else was there, among the cadre of recently retired pros, looking to forge a second career? He was the logical choice: a man who might be able to speak with authority on all three grand tours (he wore the leader's jersey in every one), relate to a British audience, and also, should the need arise, which it instantly would, when Greg Van Avermaet's name was printed on the startlist, address the issue of doping. [Van Avermaet was subject to an investigation by the Belgian cycling authorities before the Tour de Yorkshire but was cleared shortly afterwards.]

There was, of course, the potential negative impact of his self-confessed 'Marmite' status, onto which his dogmatic opponents would undoubtedly latch. There are those who have made up their mind, and whose position does not allow for Millar's reintegration into the sport, either as competitor or commentator, on any terms. But, in all likelihood, these honestly motivated detractors would find themselves outnumbered by those for whom Millar has become, despite his own personal history, a rational voice in an irrational world. I argued that we had to get Millar. And happily, we did.

He sent me an email, outlining his hopes for the new departure.

'I think more than anything what people need these days is good chat, a bit of audio entertainment over the often monotonous visuals. You'll find your racing excitement stage crescendo naturally.'

I had my doubts about that bit. But no doubt

at all as far as his input was concerned. It was my 'racing crescendo' that felt as if the clutch was sticking. Try as I might, shouting out loud at those Eurosport races with the sound turned down, I failed to convince myself, let alone our cat, to whom I was exclusively broadcasting, curled up on the couch.

'Degenkolb! Wins! Paris! Roubaix!'

I was reminded of the time on the Tour de France, in 2007, when, during live coverage of stage 21 in Paris, our truck lost power to the commentary tribune and we lost Phil and Paul. That left Gary Imlach and Chris Boardman having to commentate. The power outage lasted a long time, perilously close in fact to the point of the race, some five kilometres from the finish, when they would be forced to get hugely excited. Mercifully for both men, whose natural strengths lie in wry, downbeat observation, the line was restored to Phil and Paul to see the race home, charismatically.

'That was a relief,' I remember Chris telling me. 'Gary and I don't really do excited.'

Even then, and long before I ever thought of trying it out, I remember wondering: Could I do that?

With David Millar, the matter was more clear cut. Even though he had only once commentated for the television (a six-hour marathon alongside Hugh Porter for BBC's coverage of the World Championships in 2012), that sole appearance was still one commentary more than I had ever managed. And I did not doubt for a second that he would be alert, articulate and insightful, as well as current and informed. The only question in my mind with regard to my new co-commentator was sartorial. Which hat would he wear? Would it simply augment his visible and prodigious height advantage over me? Would I need to stand on a little box, as Gary Imlach once had to do in the company of Bradley Wiggins on the set?

Then it dawned on me that, aside from a very brief introductory piece to camera, I would no longer be required to look 'broadcast ready'. It mattered little, voice-wise, if I were dressed, not dressed, in my pyjamas or in a shell suit, or a pair of Speedos. I toyed with wearing a suit, to add gravitas.

So in the end I grew as good a beard as I could muster, finished my notes, and packed my bags. Two days before the race was to start, I jumped on a train to Yorkshire, trying to feel confident. Trying, in fact, to feel like a commentator.

I dialled the number of the *directeur sportif* of the JLT Condor team, John Herety.

'Hi, it's Ned here. Tell me, did Graham Briggs get over his ear infection?' I listened closely as he answered, and scribbled notes on the back of my hand.

Unwittingly, as the Virgin train sped through Lincolnshire, arrowing north, I had just had my defining 'Stuart Parnaby' moment. I had crossed a threshold.

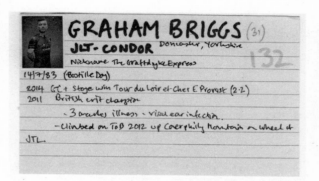

GRAHAM BRIGGS (31)
JLT-CONDOR Doncaster, Yorkshire
Nickname The Graffdyke Express
14/7/83 (Bootille Day)
2014 GC + Stage win Tour du Loir et-Cher E Provost (2.2)
2011 British crit champion
- 3 months illness - viral ear infection
- Climbed on ToB 2012 up Caerphilly Mountain on wheel of JTL.

We arrived at the start line in Scarborough about five hours before the race. That morning, out of nervous energy, I had shaved my beard off. I don't know why. I just did. It was a rubbish beard anyway.

I had made my way there in a hired Kia (a Europcar vehicle, appropriately enough). Millar arrived some short time later in a Maserati. This was to be the day's first, but not the last, reminder of our differing status.

I arranged myself in the commentary booth. It was a scaled-down unit – a kind of double decker Transformer truck parked at the finish line, with tinted windows and an air-conditioning unit permanently set to 'roasting'. Because the Tour de Yorkshire was an ASO race, the whole fleet of race vehicles had crossed the channel, and whiffed of everyday Tour de Franceness.

Outside, a fleet of red, French-numberplated

Norbert Dentressangle lorries had disgorged the barriers. There were even French-style open, up-turned mushroom-shaped *pissoirs*. And inside the commentary position (a long desk with three tellies, a bit of kit with knobs and dials, and two sets of headphone mics), there was an unexpected problem that arose directly as a result of this odd crossbred race. The bloody plugs were French.

Both David Millar and I had arrived bristling with tablets and laptops, telephones and smart-phones, all in the hope that surrounding ourselves with stuff would provide a safety net. But there was nowhere to charge them, and so we had to watch on as they slowly exhausted their batteries. A French TV technician came in to check if everything was okay. He went off in search of an adaptor, but we didn't see him again for the rest of the day. I had visions of him walking into Scarborough seafront newsagents. 'Excuse me, do you 'ave a two-pin adapter?'

'Don't think so, love. Have you tried the pet shop?'

Then, with 32 per cent left on the laptop, and with roughly 70 kilometres of the race remaining, the inevitable could be delayed no longer. After years of wondering how it's done, I was about to find out. I shuffled my notes one last time, took a sip of water, slapped Millar unexpectedly hard on the left thigh, causing him to flinch, and launched into my opening words.

All I remember, actually, is my opening word.
'So…'

That was Word One. Many thousands more were to follow that day, often in a confused jumble. But, nevertheless, there is a chance, if this all goes to plan, that many millions will pass my lips before I can call it a day, hang up the microphone, and crawl off to the armchair with the sea view at the Retirement Home For Sports Announcers.

But that was how it began.

What followed was a jumble of images: helicopter shots of exposed moorland with a long, thin line of riders buffeted by gale force winds, crawling across the landscape. Juddering moto-camera shots of riders falling in a domino pattern on a wet corner, shrouded by dappled shade from the overhanging trees. It was a constantly shifting pattern, and not at all what I was expecting, or indeed hoping, for my first live commentary.

Joining a race at 70 kilometres from the finish, especially on stage one of a three-day stage race, seemed like a perfectly benign opening gambit. Seventy kilometres, as I found out during my long springtime sojourn on the couch, listening to other commentators at work, is perfectly poised for a nap. There's nothing quite like a bike race for a midday snooze, especially if you've just had lunch. A soporific chase from a half-committed bunch, with four riders (one from each of the occasionally interchangeable Cofidis/Roompot/Topsport/CCC teams, for example) working together in balletic harmony before the inevitable catch, is sleep-inducing stuff.

I love it. The feeling of dozing off, lying on my back on the couch, letting the commentator's voice fade from view as the eyes close. Not even the rude reminders about kitchen convection fans and caffeine shampoo can stop me from going gently into that good afternoon. Seventy kilometres to go should ordinarily be the nothing zone, the dead patch, the bald spot in the middle of the day.

But no one had told Yorkshire this. At precisely the moment that the helicopter started to provide live race pictures, it was all blowing to bits on the top of the North Yorks Moors. Marcel Kittel climbed off, Ben Swift crashed and abandoned, as the main bunch split, and regrouped, split and regrouped. The race was chaos, as far as the camera lens could see, which admittedly hardly scratched the surface of what was really going on. This was my baptism.

I frowned hard for two hours, and tried as best I could to hold it all together, sometimes more coherently than at other times. Identifying riders from the head-on shot of an arrowhead Sky-driven line, or the five-abreast confusion of a half-hearted chase without portfolio was eye-openingly difficult. It wasn't helped by the fact that the riders, due to the predictable cold, had all pulled on their over-jackets,

at one fell swoop hiding their numbers from the
helicopter. It was sweat-inducing, toe-curling,
knee-jiggling stuff, and it went on and on and on.

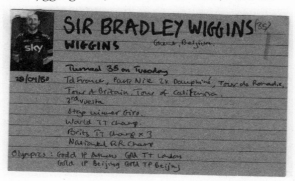

Eventually, mercifully, the race solidified from its
highly volatile liquid state into a settled group of five
riders who would contest the win. Thomas Voeckler
was among them.

Suddenly, David Millar lit up. His laid-back
laconic tone had been the cooling cucumber raita
to my prawn jalfrezi all afternoon, smoothing out
the wrinkles and moderating the hyperbole. Now,
though, he took centre stage.

This, after all, was the kind of race Millar excelled
in, particularly during the latter part of his career,
when he nearly took a solo win into Barcelona on
the 2009 Tour de France, and went one better in
2012, outwitting and outsprinting a group of five.
Now, sitting in a converted lorry in Scarborough, his

words tumbled out: a volcanic pyro-flow of tactical machinations.

'See, look, this is essence of Voeckler. He's going to drop off the back and let them think he's cooked, then hit them. He's got a Jedi force field around him.'

He called everything before it happened. It was uncanny, like he was in the heart of the race – not sitting in a sheepskin coat (he actually wore something John Motson would have envied) with a set of headphones clamped round his head. I was captivated by his instinctive reading of the unfolding drama.

In fact, I was so taken with it that I stopped watching the telly, and spun my chair round to look at him instead. This wasn't textbook TV commentary technique. But I was having one of the most interesting conversations about cycling that I'd ever had, and didn't want work to get in the way.

'Look. Sky'll hit them with a one-two. There goes Deignan. Now watch Nordhaug. There he goes.'

Somehow, and just in the nick of time, I remembered what I was being paid for, and completed the race commentary, with just a fractional wobble of uncertainty that Nordhaug was the Sky rider who won the sprint. There was 98 per cent 'Lars Petter Nordhaug!' in my voice, with just a telling two per cent of, 'Or is it Philip Deignan?'

It's not easy, this cycling lark.

At the end of it all, David Millar grabbed his things together, smacked me heartily on the back, grinned from ear to ear, and left. He had some important people from Maserati he had to schmooze.

I took my headphones off, and sat for a while with a thousand-yard stare. Everything had gone very quiet. I looked down at my desk, with notes strewn across it, like grated parmesan on a pizza. Start lists, numbers 'by *dossard*', route maps, timetables, tourist information, and everywhere the debris of the race, individual riders, plucked in paper form from the box file of the peloton and thrown onto the table for scrutiny, then pushed aside in favour of the next. I started to gather it all up, taking my time, restoring order. Tonight I would have to update my files for all the DNFs and DNSes.

Everything that I had feared and hoped for about commentating on a bike race had come to pass. Adrenalin, confusion, and wild enjoyment. One hell of a job, this.

I drove back to York. I ate a burger. I went to my room. Before falling asleep, I checked my email. I had this message from Phil Liggett.

I think you can do it and it's time for a new face. We all need chances in life and when they come —TAKE THEM!

I wish you every success.

Very best wishes, Phil

I slept well that night. I was one of them.

Ned Boulting first reported on the Tour de France for ITV in 2003, and has been on the race ever since. At least that's what it feels like.

2

Andy McGrath tells the story of a small French team that was awarded a wild card for the 1997 Tour de France at short notice.

La Mutuelle de Seine-et-Marne were not just underdogs, they were minnows swimming against the tide.

One by one, they dropped out of the race until only two were left to make it to Paris.

AND THEN THERE WERE TWO

BY ANDY McGRATH

Disneyland Paris is meant to be more fun than this. In a hotel room in the sprawling entertainment resort, on the eve of the 1997 Tour de France's final stage, Stéphane Cueff was sharing his worries with remaining team-mate Dominique Rault.

How would everyone else perceive them and their team, riding down the Champs-Élysées to finish the Tour with just two riders? And how had this happened? He wasn't just questioning the last fortnight, during which Mutuelle de Seine-et-Marne had shed most of their starting line-up, but what on earth was going on with professional cycling at the time?

Then again, it was a big relief. He was at the end of his tether, but he and Rault had made it – the only survivors from the nine-man team, mostly comprising Tour virgins, that started the event.

Simply gaining entry to cycling's biggest race was a coup for La Mutuelle de Seine-et-Marne – the minnows of the race. Their budget was six times lower than most of their rivals. They started the 1997 Tour as virtual unknowns; by the end of the race,

much of France had heard about, and sympathised
with, the plucky battlers in blue and white.

Their record of two finishers and a handful of
top-10 stage finishes was one of the worst since
trade teams were introduced to the Tour de France
in 1969. But mere results don't come anywhere close
to telling the wild-card team's remarkable story. As
the saying goes, it's about the journey, not the desti-
nation — and La Mutuelle de Seine-et-Marne had one
hell of a ride.

* * *

La Mutuelle de Seine-et-Marne was a health insurance company comprising 200 employees, based on
the southern outskirts of Paris. Its director general,
Daniel Gourdet, was a cycling aficionado who wanted to reinforce the business's position in its regional
heartland south-east of the capital, while also getting its name out to middle France. TV advertising
was too pricey and run-of-the-mill. He convinced
the company president that backing a professional
cycling team was the way to promote the business; it
was an open, accessible sport and they could link it
up to their principles.

The company had already dipped its toe in the
water by co-sponsoring top French amateur squad
US Créteil in 1994, and they agreed to stump up the
cash to become a UCI-accredited professional team,

using the Parisian team structure as a nucleus. Chief team manager Yvon Sanquer masterminded the operation with Jacky Lachevre as deputy. They didn't set out to conquer the cycling world; instead, the team's philosophy was to nurture young French talent.

Setting out with a dozen-strong line-up almost entirely made up of first-year professionals, they had a tough time learning the ropes.

'It was another world,' Gilles Maignan says. The powerful *rouleur* was one of six promising US Créteil talents who turned professional with the team; others joined from various French amateur squads.

'The difference was enormous,' Maignan recalls of their first big race – the 1995 Paris-Nice. 'The way of racing was completely different, the speed was a lot faster and the rhythm wasn't anything like in the amateur ranks, where it goes all out from the gun and the attacking doesn't stop. Adapting was quite difficult.'

At least the feeling was mutual.

'We were all in the same boat. We lacked experience,' Jean-François Anti, another man to move up from US Créteil, says. 'In very little time, I went from being a spectator to a character in the race. I watched Paris-Roubaix on TV one year; the next I was lining up on the start line. It was tough mentally.'

Mutuelle de Seine-et-Marne raced almost exclusively on the French circuit. Though they gained entry into prestigious races such as Paris-Nice,

Paris-Roubaix and the Dauphiné Libéré, they were
habitually fighting teams with far bigger names and
means. Their first victory didn't arrive until August
1995.

It wasn't purely inexperience, size or lack of
ability keeping them well down the pecking order,
though. These were bad years of cheating. There
has since been evidence of systemic doping in the
Festina, Gewiss and US Postal teams in the late
1990s and use of the blood booster erythropoietin
(EPO) was prevalent in the peloton. With no direct
test for the drug available, at the turn of 1997, the
UCI imposed a 50 per cent haematocrit (red blood
cell count) limit. The penalty for exceeding that in
a mandatory test was a 15-day suspension. It was
designed as a health measure to deter cheating, but
appears to have been used as a depraved yardstick,
with some riders testing their blood to see how close
to that magic half-century they could get.

The sordid pharmaceutical revolution ratcheting
up speed and shaking up results was something the
Mutuelle riders could not ignore.

'We know that there were a lot of riders who
cheated,' road captain Jean-Philippe Dojwa says. 'It
wasn't our policy in Mutuelle de Seine-et-Marne.
Our boss Daniel Gourdet told us: "I don't want
doping; maybe results will be hard to come by, but
it's not a big deal. I want a clean and honest team,"'
Dojwa says. 'Monsieur Gourdet knew perfectly how

it worked in cycling at the time, but there wasn't a results-at-all-costs philosophy. That suited me well.'

With many team members knowing one another since their amateur days in the early '90s, they could rely on a close bond to get through the challenges.

'It was a family team; there was no pressure like in the big squads,' Laurent Pillon says.

At the turn of 1997, the leading 16 teams in the UCI world rankings gained automatic qualification for the 1997 Tour de France. This included powerhouses of the scene such as Telekom, home to defending Tour de France champion Bjarne Riis, Festina and their French star Richard Virenque, and ONCE, who possessed the world's top-ranked two riders, Laurent Jalabert and Alex Zülle. As expected, Mutuelle de Seine-et-Marne were not even close.

Their only hope was to gain entry through the wild-card system. The Tour de France organisers had six discretionary picks to hand to teams, and there were ten outfits in the running. La Mutuelle de Seine-et-Marne were seen as unlikely candidates given their average showings and second-division status. They had until June to show their worth; their big races became auditions.

As the season gathered pace, they remained in the running partly through the mediocrity of several better-known rivals. Italian team Scrigno – 17th in the rankings – offered little, and Asics captain Claudio Chiappucci, second in the 1990 and 1992 Tour de France, was going like a bag of spanners, making headlines for exceeding the haematocrit level at the Tour of Romandy rather than winning anything.

La Mutuelle de Seine-et-Marne struck a timely blow at the Midi Libre stage race in south-west France. On stage four, their Canadian sprinter Gord Fraser beat Frédéric Moncassin and Adriano Baffi to win in Montpellier. It suggested that they could be more than pack fodder at the Tour de France.

There was one more stage race – one final opportunity to convince the Tour de France organisers: the Dauphiné Libéré – a week-long Alpine event traditionally used as a final sharpener by Tour-bound riders.

The team's results were decent, but unspectacular. Fraser sprinted to sixth on one stage, and Gilles Maignan finished seventh in a long time trial among the sport's stars. Some people already reckoned that wouldn't be enough: during the final stage, French cycling television commentator Jean-René Godart announced live on air that he didn't think this plucky, courageous little team would make the Tour cut. Later, while waiting at the airport for the flight home, La Mutuelle's team captain Jean-Philippe Dojwa had a lively exchange of views with Godart, annoyed that he publicly said such things without knowing the truth.

Maybe Dojwa had gotten wind of the forthcoming decision. Because, despite what they lacked in

big-name riders, budget, experience, results and
ranking points, Mutuelle de Seine-et-Marne had one
decisive thing going for them: they were French.
Their kit – blue shorts, white jersey with blue on the
shoulders and red trim on the collar – even faintly
resembled the tricolore flag.

Two days after the finish of the Dauphiné, the
Tour wild-card picks were announced. Lotto, US
Postal, Kelme and Mercatone Uno were selected,
alongside two French squads: BigMat-Auber 93 and
Mutuelle de Seine-et-Marne.

The director of the Société du Tour de France,
Jean-Marie Leblanc, copped a lot of flak for
choosing two unheralded French squads, languishing
outside the top 30 in the UCI world rankings.

'If we had taken on Italian riders and teams rather
than the French ones, we would have had 30 French
riders against 75 Italians at the start of the race.
Given the state of French cycling – I would say the
gap between French and Italian riders isn't as great as
it was a year ago – it would seem to me that having
40 French riders at the start is the minimum we could
have,' Leblanc said at the time. 'As the Société du
Tour de France, we have looked towards youth rather
than experience.'

La Mutuelle de Seine-et-Marne's riders and
management were delighted, but ill-prepared. The
announcement of the wild-card teams had been
pushed back until June 17 – two-and-a-half weeks

before the start of the Tour. To put it into perspective: for the contemporary race, the few wild-card picks are usually made by April, allowing ample time for the preparation of riders and logistics.

This delayed news, while welcome, was akin to an opera singer at the Royal Albert Hall being told they were due on stage in 15 minutes, having already done weeks of matinee shows.

'A good part of the team had already given everything getting selected for the team. The energy that had been spent before was considerable. That's another reason we had a lot of difficulties in the Tour de France,' Stéphane Cueff says. 'Other teams had most of their selection picked one or two months before; we only had ours confirmed the week before the start of the Tour. So the psychological preparation was rather lacking, too.'

Cueff's was one of the first names on the team sheet of manager Yvon Sanquer, who waited until the French national championships, a week before the start of the Tour de France, to pick the ninth and final man. Immediately after the race, Sanquer told Jean-François Anti that he was in.

'It was joy; I can't describe that feeling adequately. Which pro cyclist doesn't dream of doing the Tour de France? There's not one, especially if you're French,' Anti says. He had grown up riding with Pédale Combs-la-Villaise – the same cycling club as his hero and two-time Tour de France winner

Laurent Fignon. 'Then afterwards, you think about it all. Once that joy has passed, you start reflecting, and there starts to be apprehension, a bit of fear. Because it was a journey of discovery for us.'

* * *

Mutuelle de Seine-et-Marne were at the bottom of the 1997 Tour de France start list – the 20th of the 22 teams racing.

Directeur sportif: Yvon Sanquer
201 – Jean-Philippe Dojwa
202 – Jean-François Anti
203 – Stéphane Cueff
204 – David Delrieu
205 – Gordon Fraser
206 – Claude Lamour
207 – Gilles Maignan
208 – Laurent Pillon
209 – Dominique Rault

Road captains Jean-Philippe Dojwa and Laurent Pillon were the only riders with past Tour de France experience. As a 25 year old in 1993, Dojwa had finished 15th overall and best Frenchman, which piled pressure on his young shoulders. Though there was no chance he'd be challenging Bjarne Riis and company for the yellow jersey, he was La Mutuelle's man for a decent finish in the general classification.

Elsewhere, sprinter Gord Fraser had caught the eye, claiming several competitive placings throughout the season.

'He's La Mutuelle's only hope for a stage win,' was *Cycling Weekly*'s assessment in their 1997 Tour de France preview edition.

Remarkably, two men from the same Breton village were included in the line-up, too. Fast finisher Claude Lamour and *rouleur-baroudeur* Stéphane Cueff were born in Landivisiau, four days apart.

'They called us the two brothers,' Lamour says. 'We were at school together, we started racing together as kids, we moved to Paris together and we turned pro together, too.'

In three years, Mutuelle de Seine-et-Marne had gone from being an amateur French cycling team to racing the sport's most prestigious event. It was a short decampment from their south Parisian base up the motorway to the start of the 1997 Tour de France in Rouen. Once there, the squad's eyes were opened to the task at hand.

'Even the team presentation of the Tour, two days before the start, was grandiose. That was the first realisation that we were at an event with completely different dimensions,' Gilles Maignan says.

The squad's modest six-million-franc budget – around 1.5 million euros in modern money – paled in comparison to their rivals', most of whom had five times that amount; their little camper van was dwarfed by the mighty buses of the leading teams. They were literally the small fry of the 1997 Tour bunch: their 161-centimetre Breton rider Dominique Rault earned La Mutuelle a rare mention in the dispatches for measuring up as the shortest rider in the Tour peloton at the pre-race medical checks.

The race started ominously for one of the team's most experienced members, Laurent Pillon. He went out for a training ride on the eve of the prologue, crashed and got bad road rash (it was far from the last time he would hit the deck that month). When Pillon returned to his hotel room, his possessions were gone.

'Someone had stolen my wallet, my ID and what little money I had, so I had to go down to the police station on the evening before the prologue,' Pillon says.

In the prologue itself, Chris Boardman claimed victory, while Gilles Maignan finished just inside the top 30, inspired by the masses on the route bellowing support for the unknown French wild-card team.

The first road stage between Rouen and Forges-les-Eaux was hectic. Pillon was back in the wars, crashing in the neutralised zone before the race had officially started, then two more times during the stage. Tour contender Alex Zülle of ONCE was one of the big favourites to squander his chances, coming down in a pile-up near the finish.

Gord Fraser dodged the crashes and came to the fore, finishing seventh to Mario Cipollini. Again, this was a mismatch: Cipollini, the best sprinter of the age, had practically the entire Saeco team at his disposal to chase down breakaways and then force the pace as the finish approached. Jean-François Anti was Fraser's only helper, doing his best to keep the North American near the front.

On the following stage to Vire, Jean-Philippe Dojwa briefly went up the road with one thing in his mind. Hailing from nearby Elbeuf, he knew his other half was standing on the roadside near the Pont de Brotonne. As Tour tradition dictated, the bunch had slowed to allow him a few seconds to lead the race, stop and embrace her. There was just one problem.

'There were so many people on the side of the road. I looked and looked, but I never saw her.'

Dojwa had to remount, having missed his planned kiss.

Near the end of the stage, Gilles Maignan attacked and got into a short breakaway with Laurent Jalabert and Erik Breukink. 'Jalabert was world number one, Breukink was a super rider, too – and then there was me, virtually a neo-pro, escaping with them. It's a strong memory, although my legs certainly knew about it afterwards,' he says.

Claude Lamour capped the day by finishing seventh in the concluding bunch sprint. *Les petits Bleus* were punching above their weight. On day five, as Cédric Vasseur claimed the yellow jersey of race leader with a lone breakaway to La Châtre, Stéphane Cueff slipped away in the closing kilometres with ten others and finished eighth. But with the Pyrenees looming, fatigue was starting to show, and the team would pay for its exuberance. Even attempting to get into a breakaway can have an effect on the body further down the line.

'When you're young and don't know the Tour de France, you can be intoxicated by the race,' Dojwa says. 'You can get a bit too fired up without thinking that it's three weeks long. When you have done it before, you learn to save your energy, to rest whenever you can.'

And in Maignan's opinion, the weight of media interest only contributes to the tiredness.

'There were all these journalists who were interested in us because we were the Tour's little team,' he explains. 'TV, radio, written press; we were asked questions in the morning before the stage, afterwards at the finish, then someone would phone up in the evening. It was all new to us, so we were super happy... But in the end, I think we paid for it.'

They were the naïfs of the Tour, unaccustomed to this different dimension where everything from the crowds to the hotels seemed larger. Just ask Claude Lamour. One night, he got lost trying to find his room in particularly labyrinthine accommodation. He knew that his room-mate Dominique Rault was having a massage somewhere on site, but had no way of contacting him, this being years before the age of smartphones. Every attempt to locate his room would end up with Lamour emerging, perplexed, in a different part of the hotel. Unable to find an employee to help, Lamour spent an hour searching.

'Although I could laugh about it afterwards, it wasn't so funny at the time,' he says.

La Mutuelle de Seine-et-Marne lost Gord Fraser on stage nine – the first big day in the mountains over the Soulor, Tourmalet and Aspin to Val-Louron. Their sprinter completed the stage, but was eliminated by the time cut – the rule which stipulates that riders must finish within a certain percentage of the winner's time each day to stay in the race.

Twenty-four hours later, the unfancied team from the Seine-et-Marne were briefly leading the Tour de France. Their big moment came on stage ten from Luchon to Andorra – a 252-kilometre day over five mountains before a final haul to Arcalis.

As the race's favourites prevaricated, Jean-Philippe Dojwa seized his opportunity, accelerating over the penultimate climb, the Col d'Ordino, to lead the Tour onto the final climb to Arcalis by a minute. It was a move of panache that won him the day's combativity prize, and is still occasionally mentioned to him by fans nearly 20 years on.

'Behind me, at that moment, you had so many big names and great champions. For this little team, to find itself in front in the most beautiful stage of the Tour was incredible,' Dojwa recalls. 'I told myself to give it everything.'

All round France, people were tuning in, wondering who Mutuelle de Seine-et-Marne were and whether Dojwa could take an unlikely win. The Telekom prodigy Jan Ullrich tore up the fairytale script, though, flying past seven kilometres from the top, making his first moves towards Tour de France victory.

'I had the impression that I was being passed by a motorbike,' remembers Dojwa.

The double entendre works: several of the top performers of that 1997 Tour were souped up. In 2013, Ullrich admitted to doping, undergoing blood procedures with notorious Spanish doctor Eufemiano Fuentes in the mid-noughties.

'Almost everybody back then took performance-enhancing substances. I didn't take anything which the others were not taking,' Ullrich told *Focus* magazine. Fellow podium finishers Richard Virenque and Marco Pantani also doped during their careers.

While La Mutuelle often couldn't compete with the physical, pharmaceutical or financial firepower of some other teams, they were advanced in other aspects. Yvon Sanquer, who looked more professor than cycling manager with his glasses and trim blonde hair, had the team wearing Polar heart-rate monitors, primitive by today's standards but cutting-edge tech then. He would spend his evenings inputting their data into the computer.

Sanquer was the tougher, more forensic figure to second *directeur sportif* Jacky Lachevre's paternalist. Several riders told me that the pair had completely different personalities.

'Jacky was more detached; Yvon was the *patron*, so he was a bit more tense. I think he took all the pressure [from the sponsors] and did his utmost to not put it on us,' Maignan says.

From the high of Dojwa's daring escape, the fatigue began to bite. Ten days into the race, most of the team was entering unprecedented territory. Even the Mutuelle camper van was feeling the strain, its motor cutting out at the end of one stage.

On the 11th stage to Perpignan, Jean-François Anti was the next Mutuelle rider to exit.

'I made an error of youth. I went back to look for bidons to give to my team-mates. Unfortunately, the moment I did that, the bunch accelerated brutally. I found myself among the team cars, all alone. I couldn't get back to the peloton,' he says.

The kilometres ticked by and he fought on, 40 minutes behind the head of the race, certain to be eliminated by the time cut. But there was another cruel twist: the gendarmes, keeping the roads closed to traffic on the outskirts of Perpignan, grew impatient and demanded that the organisers stopped tardy riders.

'Even if you're outside the Tour de France time limit, you have the right to finish the race. I knew I was going to be eliminated, but I wanted to complete it for my honour,' Anti says. 'I was stopped by a commissaire; it wasn't a dramatic thing. But I was the first rider in the Tour de France to be stopped like that – and possibly the last one, too.'

Within months, the tall *rouleur* went from the Tour de France peloton to quitting cycling altogether. Doping was one of the chief reasons; he was Anti by name, anti by nature.

'I completed half a Tour de France and three years as a pro because I decided to not do that... I didn't endanger my health. Cycling was an exceptional adventure with great highs and difficult moments. When you see your career doesn't match the heights of your dreams, it's not always easy. But it was my choice. After the cycling, there remains a man. I'm prouder to have not doped and had a little career than to have cheated and had a glittering one,' he says.

The stage 12 time trial in Saint-Étienne showed the ridiculous gulf in performance. Jan Ullrich routed the field, beating everyone by three minutes over the 55 kilometre route. His closest challenger was Richard Virenque. The best-placed Mutuelle de Seine-et-Marne rider that day was Claude Lamour, nine minutes behind.

Stéphane Cueff recalls sitting in a hotel room

with the remainder of the team afterwards, chatting about the incredible feats they were riding against.

'That showed the big difficulty of that year's Tour. Physically, everyone was at their peak, virtually all the time,' he says.

As the Tour headed into the Alps, Mutuelle de Seine-et-Marne lost three riders on one day. Stage 14 was a short, sadistic brute, taking the riders over the *hors-catégorie* horrors of the Glandon, Madeleine and up to the finish at Courchevel.

An exhausted Maignan abandoned at the feed zone.

'Festina were having a festival on the Col du Glandon, all on the front of the bunch going *à bloc*, and I was among the first to be dropped,' he recalls. 'I preferred to stop rather than finishing completely burned out. I'd always seen riders on TV crying because they abandoned the Tour. That wasn't the case for me at all: I was so tired that it was a relief for it to be over.

'When I got home, my morale was so worn out that I didn't want to go back. I thought, "I've done the Tour once; it's too hard." I changed my mind later, but that's how I felt at the time,' he says.

Meanwhile, Claude Lamour had been fretting about that stage since before the race had left Rouen. He barely slept the night before through anxiety.

'I had cracked mentally,' he says.

Days before, he had made the basic error of

burning himself out trying to keep up with the peloton, unaware there was a *gruppetto* of 70 riders behind
him. It burned some of his last energy reserves.

'That day to Courchevel, I was out the back and
out the window.'

Team-mate Laurent Pillon, also off the back,
missed out on staying in the Tour by just 30 seconds.
He crashed again – the fifth fall of his luckless Tour
– while taking risks on the descent of the Madeleine
to make up ground. He burst into tears at the top
of Courchevel, packed his bags and caught the TGV
back north the next morning.

'I'd never quit a Tour de France before; it was
the worst thing that could happen,' Pillon says. 'After
I got home, I didn't watch that year's Tour any more
because I was a bit disgusted. It was the lowest
moment in my career.'

Pillon was sad to not be reinstated given the
remarkable circumstances that had unfolded. As
Richard Virenque rocketed to victory, the rest of the
Mutuelle de Seine-et-Marne team finished in a large
group just half a minute ahead of Pillon, comprising
94 of the 171 riders. It crossed the line 36 minutes
and 56 seconds behind Virenque, well outside the 12
per cent time limit of 32 minutes and 25 seconds.
If the commissaires hadn't bent the rules – to avoid
the farce of having a 60-strong bunch for the race's
final week – two-thirds of the field would have gone
home, including the entire Mutuelle de Seine-et-

Marne, Gan and MG-Technogym teams.

Dojwa had been the only rider on the team feeling halfway decent up to this point, flirting with the top 30 overall. But injury did for him too.

'Two stages before that, I was super; two days later, I couldn't even turn the pedals,' he says. 'I think the staff made a little error. We changed to Look bikes just before the start of the Tour, perhaps for the promotion of the brand. I think the size of the frame I got was a bit different, and with the repetitive efforts of the race, I got tendonitis in my knee.

'In the Tour de France, you can't have little problems. A small issue quickly grows with fatigue and accumulated efforts.'

Dojwa abandoned on stage 15, and David Delrieu, who had shown ability in the Pyrenees, pulled out the following day, unable to shake off tendonitis.

And then there were two: Stéphane Cueff and Dominique Rault. La Mutuelle de Seine-et-Marne was no longer a team, and more of a Breton duo.

The rest of the team called Rault '*Le Bûcheron*' – The Woodcutter – for his punchy, power-packed style. He was one of the jokers of the group, but there were precious few wise-cracks flying around now most of La Mutuelle had gone home.

'Does it make you happy fitting the whole team inside this one car?' Cueff asked their driver on the morning of stage 17. There were now more team cars than team riders, and far more bikes than they knew what to do with. At least logistics were simpler: many of the staff went home, surplus to requirements.

Was it lonely for them?

'Yes,' Cueff replies. 'Dominique is a very strong character, too; he was not going to give up. He was always pushing himself to the limit. I think you had to remember the others [who had left the race] and then show that we were still there. It wasn't easy, but we made it.'

That's Cueff's quiet determination for you. When asked if he ever thought of abandoning, he replies: 'No, never. It was out of the question. I'd sooner die on the bike.'

He remembers sitting in a hotel room with Rault in Disneyland Paris on the eve of the final stage, wondering how they would be treated as the Mutuelle de Seine-et-Marne duo riding the famous circuit of the capital. He was worried about what it meant for cycling at the time, too.

'There was a big question mark. We knew that a lot of negative things were going on. Not being part of that system made us ask a lot of questions, certainly. But I have no regrets now,' Cueff says.

When the final moments in Paris came around and the bunch hit the Champs-Élysées, his anxiety melted away.

'It was magical. It's every rider's dream to finish

one Tour de France at the very least,' Cueff, who now owns a bike shop a few kilometres from the finish line in Paris, says.

Dominique Rault finished the 1997 Tour de France in 83rd place, just over three hours behind winner Jan Ullrich; Cueff was 138th and second-to-last. The celebration was underwhelming: they had a small dinner after the race with some returning team members, who were still downcast from their experiences.

While finishing with two riders was an anomaly, La Mutuelle were not alone in shedding team members. It was a particularly attritional edition of the race: Lotto and Roslotto-ZG Mobili limped into Paris with three finishers; wild-card outfit Big-Mat-Auber 93 had four.

Doping had plenty to do with the unrelenting speed, recovery and psychological advantage. Given what we know from the intervening years of scandals, admissions and retroactive doping positives, many of the names in the top ten make for grim reading: the likes of Ullrich, Pantani, Riis and Francesco Casagrande are synonymous with a dirty era, but all were feted at the time. Most of France was particularly giddy over runner-up Richard Virenque and his attacking riding.

'I think that our two riders who finished [Rault and Cueff] pushed themselves to their limits – they'd given everything. They deserved more press than all the winners because they did the Tour naturally. But for the media, it's the Tour de France, and only the winners count. And we don't talk much about the helpers. *C'est la vie*,' Laurent Pillon says.

* * *

You could imagine that the bosses providing the team's budget weren't laughing at the lacklustre performance. But, inversely, the company name had been getting out there and Mutuelle de Seine-et-Marne reaped the rewards in media attention. Awareness of the brand soared; 36 per cent knew the company name at the finish, three times more than at the race start.

'For the same result from advertising campaigns, we would have had to invest three times more money,' director general Daniel Gourdet told *Le Petit Parisien* in 2012.

Delighted with the reaction, La Mutuelle also sponsored the team for the 1998 season, which became the squad's best year so far. Francisque Teyssier claimed the GP des Nations time trial, Stéphane Cueff won the GP d'Isbergues and Gilles Maignan took the French national time trial title. None were the same scale as the Tour de France but they were all tough races and for a small team they were significant victories.

'I think doing the Tour de France brought the

majority of us on because the results completely
changed the next season,' Maignan says. 'We began
winning good races.'

But as they pursued another wild-card entry for
the 1998 Tour de France, the company was rocked
by an unexpected attack. In early June, at the cycling
team's humble headquarters in Melun, a parcel bomb
exploded in the face of a member of staff. Despite
serious injuries, he was able to inform the security
services, who put out the small fire.

'Two days before the [football] World Cup starts
[in France], security is reinforced everywhere, and
a cycling team is the victim of an attack! It's mad.
We've never received threats. I'm flabbergasted,'
Gourdet said at the time.

The squad subsequently raced at the Dauphiné
Libéré with a group of personal protectors.

'We went on our bikes to sign on with the bodyguards, we went to the toilet with the bodyguards…
All day long, morning to night, bodyguards,'
remembers Jean-Philippe Dojwa. 'It was pretty
incredible.'

It was probably for the best that Mutuelle de
Seine-et-Marne missed out on 1998 Tour de France
selection. The Festina Affair flared up, confirming
systemic doping in one of the sport's top teams.
Police raided the hotels of many other squads;
several went on to quit the race in protest. The Tour
limped to the finish, with professional cycling and its

flagship race tarnished.

It is difficult to decontextualise the 1997 Tour from cheating. 'The doping cast enormous shadows. I think that was already one of the terrible years of doping,' Cueff says.

When asked if it annoyed him, he responds: 'No – that was my era. Each one has its problems.'

While it is tempting to suggest La Mutuelle was one of the clean teams at the 1997 Tour – for what it's worth, several of its riders are adamant that they raced it without doping – it's impossible to ascertain.

'I can't say for sure, but I'm 80 per cent sure the team was clean,' Jean-François Anti says. 'We only had two riders at the finish! That explains everything: we were better than a lot. But we weren't doped.'

La Mutuelle de Seine-et-Marne pulled out of sponsorship at the end of 1998, but it remained a team with a heart and an unusual social responsibility. Boss Daniel Gourdet gave his charges months of notice to find new squads for the following season.

According to Jean-Philippe Dojwa, Gourdet even proposed to help riders to find other teams and offered a hand reintegrating those who were retiring into the working world.

'I said to myself, "It's time to stop – I'm going to change lives,"' Dojwa says. 'Daniel Gourdet even offered to get me a job at Mutuelle de Seine-et-Marne. I found that comprehensive – really super.'

He turned it down though, not wanting to go

from an outdoorsy career to office life.

Gourdet was as good as his word for rehousing other riders and a core of Mutuelle riders remained together for another season. Laurent Pillon says that Gourdet struck a deal with Didier Paindaveine, the general manager of the small Belgian team Home Market-Ville de Charleroi. Five riders – Pillon, Stéphane Cueff, neo-pro Jérôme Bernard, Frédéric Gabriel and Charles Guilbert – rode there in 1999.

'I respect Monsieur Gourdet enormously,' Jean-François Anti says. 'He really wanted to do something for cycling. The only thing that limited his action was the size of the business: La Mutuelle de Seine-et-Marne was too small for modern cycling. With more money, I think he'd have liked to do something bigger.'

As the team dissolved, the boys in blue and white were scattered around the peloton. Anti and Jean-Philippe Dojwa retired. Gilles Maignan, who had emerged as an excellent time triallist, signed for Ag2r Prévoyance, where he would enjoy the best results of his career, winning a stage in the Midi Libre, another French national time trial title and the Tour Down Under – the latter now one of professional cycling's leading stage races. But he didn't forget La Mutuelle de Seine-et-Marne in a hurry.

'It's always sad when an adventure has to stop. I had been there since the beginning and we had all started from zero. We were all practically neo-pros:

the directors, the staff — they were like us.

'If I was able to achieve what I did with other teams, it's thanks to La Mutuelle and Yvon Sanquer. If he hadn't been there, I don't think I'd have been a pro rider. The team was my last chance.'

The squad proved successful in its goal of developing riders, sending several onto top-tier French teams. David Delrieu finished the 2000 Tour de France alongside Maignan at Ag2r. Meanwhile, Claude Lamour moved to Cofidis, and the hardy Dominique Rault joined BigMat-Auber 93.

Perhaps the biggest success befell team manager Yvon Sanquer. One moment he was over-seeing minnows, the next he was handed control of Festina, charged with getting the disgraced squad on the right track.

* * *

So, 18 summers on, where are the Mutuelle nine? Jean-François Anti owns a camping site in the Seine-et-Marne and even does the occasional race. Claude Lamour is a salesman in Roscoff. Many of the others have stayed in the cycling milieu. Stéphane Cueff runs a Parisian bike shop and Jean-Philippe Dojwa is a sales representative for a bike brand.

Ironically for a man who swore off the Tour de France after his abortive debut, Gilles Maignan works with Tour organisers ASO as a driver for race director Christian Prudhomme.

Laurent Pillon has been team manager of French amateur team ESEG Douai since the turn of the century, while Gord Fraser is a *directeur sportif* with Canadian team Silber, and has his own cycling coaching company. The exact whereabouts of Dominique Rault and David Delrieu are unclear, however.

Their 1997 Tour de France campaign is now a footnote in history. All the Mutuelle riders have faded into the deepest recesses of cycling fans' minds; even their own memories of the race are becoming hazier.

As for Mutuelle de Seine-et-Marne, that has disappeared into the ether, too. It was swallowed up in a merger, becoming part of Mutuelle Blue.

* * *

Why do some of us gravitate towards the underdog? Maybe it piques our innate sense of fairness in the world, serving as a form of compensation. Maybe it feeds our optimism for life in general.

'If the strongest win all the battles, there's no hope for the rest of us, is there?' said the writer Malcolm Gladwell.

In this case, the David didn't conquer the Goliaths of cycling: it was predominantly the other way round. But they had moments in the ascendancy and, though outclassed, they were unbowed.

Mutuelle de Seine-et-Marne were arguably the last great underdog to make the cut. They are a symbol of a more romantic era when the Tour de France and professional cycling wasn't quite so ruthless, when the sport's biggest race could be undertaken on a wing, a prayer, a budget of a few million francs and a dream. Undoubtedly, they also had a rare, different vocation to the rival teams. Their *raison d'être* was as much about providing a pathway from amateur level to the sport's summit as winning lots of races.

'It's a completely different story to the likes of Team Sky,' team manager Yvon Sanquer says in his deep voice. 'With the internationalisation and evolution of cycling, I think it'll be harder for there to ever be another team like ours in the Tour de France.'

Nowadays, virtually every team is selected on merit and the gap in quality between the strongest squads and wild-card teams has narrowed. As a spectacle, the Tour de France is better, closer, more meritocratic and (here's hoping) less affected by doping.

But it's nice to remind ourselves that sport is about much more than winning or losing. For La Mutuelle de Seine-et-Marne, finishing was enough.

Andy McGrath is the managing editor of *Rouleur* and a former reporter for *Cycle Sport* and *Cycling Weekly*. He has covered every Tour de France since 2010. He would love to get La Mutuelle de Seine-et-Marne's Tour team back together for a reunion at a Buffalo Grill.

3

Vernon Vurner's life changed for the better when his son, Cody, introduced him – although not personally – to Lance Armstrong.

Robert Millar shows us just how much of an impression the Texan made on our mild-mannered man from North Carolina.

DEAR LANCE

BY ROBERT MILLAR

The Vurner Family, Biscoe, North Carolina
November 4th, 1996

Dear Lance,

From all the Vurner Klan here in North Carolina
may we wish a speedy recovery from your illness. I
know it seems a bit strange to be writing something
quite personal to someone I don't know so I'll
briefly try to explain. My son Cody has turned into
your greatest fan. He has been following your career
ever since he came back from school last year with a
project about minority sports in the US.

I have to admit I never thought much about
cycling. I never really knew it existed as a proper
sport – well, not compared to baseball and
football, so when my youngest came home and
announced he'd chosen Lance Armstrong and
cycling, we did wonder what was he was on about.

I thought for a moment you might be related to
that other Armstrong but I guess I know better now
that Cody has educated me better. Children can be

so engrossed at his age (he's ten by the way) and
ever since that day he's been following you with an
intense interest that borders on the scary at times.
He's got so many posters and results stuck on his
bedroom wall, it's unbelievable, and he's been really
upset to read that you are poorly. I said to him he
ought to write to you offering his support but being
a bit shy he's made his dad do it.

So here I am trying to put into words what Cody
wants to say. He usually just shouts, 'Go Lance!' at
the TV whenever he catches a cycling report with
you in it but, since you're in treatment, we thought
you might need something a bit more personal.

I was trying to explain to Cody that maybe you
might not be the same person after all the medica-
tions and procedures and that it didn't really matter
if you weren't because any time with your family
and friends can be enough to fill a person's life.

But I guess he's still a bit young to take that in.
In fact, he discounted the idea of Lance Armstrong
being just a normal guy. He said you would be
back and you would be great. I think he had been
watching Terminator or something, but you have to
admire the sentiment and innocence of children as
they often see things we adults don't. So there you
have it, Lance – you have to get better, and all of us
Vurners will be rooting for you.

God bless, and get well soon,

Vernon, Cody & all the Vurners

The Vurner Family, Biscoe, North Carolina
October 10th, 1998

Dear Lance,

We are so thankful that you're back, Lance – healthy, strong and being a great example to everyone that cancer doesn't need to be the end of your ambitions, even when you want to be a competitive sportsman. You really are an example of what good things can be done nowadays by America's best doctors and hospitals.

Cody tells me you are on an American team now, which is how he says it should be, and you'll be way better than if you had stayed with those two-faced Frenchies at that Cofodis team. Did they really sack you because you were ill? You know that's so typical of the French – not even grateful that we saved them during WW2 and so insular that they think only they know how to do things. We had a guy, Pierre, from France working with our company and he was a useless piece of junk. Always saying he was tired or needing a holiday and that we ought to be striking for more of everything. I think he was one of those lazy social justice idiots that wanted the world given to him. He sure didn't fit in with the rest of us with his two-hour lunch breaks and hands so soft they got blisters carrying a cardboard box. He was in the wrong job. I don't think I told you last time I wrote that I'm an air

conditioning engineer, so if you ever need some
maintenance or installation stuff doing then let me
know. I know it's hardly likely but the offer is there
and I could bring Cody to meet you. He'd be so
surprised he'd probably be speechless which would
be a first given all we ever hear about is Lance
Armstrong this and that. He's a great kid.

Why isn't he writing? Well he's out working so
he can save up and buy a better bicycle. Yeah, that's
right – he's cycling now on an old bike given to us
by a friend, but you know how kids are: it has to be
better, shinier, newer, so he's got two jobs going
now. He's crazy on his old bike as it is, riding it to
school, into town – everywhere, in fact, so God
knows what he'll be like when he's got something
with proper gears and wheels. I suppose it's better
than being a useless bum like so many kids his age.

And it's thanks to you, Lance, that he's on
the right track. So you Go Lance – you show the
French and the rest of those Euro types just how
great Americans can be.

God bless, and take care,

Vern, Cody & all the Vurners

The Vurner Family, Biscoe, North Carolina
September 2nd, 1999

Dear Lance,

What a guy! You showed them, Lance – your first
Tour de France and you well and truly proved what
someone can do when they have the right attitude.
You've beaten cancer, Lance, and now you can beat
all those guys who have said you were washed up.
Cody's been ecstatic ever since ESPN showed that
first race with you in that yellow top. What do they
call it – the *maillot jaune*? Jeez, I had to check my
spelling as my French isn't exactly great, but never
mind – I'm sure that being such a great guy, Lance,
you'll forgive my mistakes.

Cody even got me to sit down and watch some
of the racing and, damn, it looks exciting.

You know you could get hurt doing some of
those downhills at the speeds you guys are going,
and those daily finishes when you all arrive together
look dangerous. But, hey, I guess it's just another
day's work when it's your job. And what a job you're
doing, Lance – you dominated those guys. Not only
that, your US Postal team dominated the race and
showed everyone just how America got where it
is today. It got me thinking about your story. You
know, with the cancer and the comeback and now
winning the world's toughest bicycle race, you really
are unique and you could become a modern

example of our great American forebears.

Seriously you can.

And you're a dad too now? Hey – join the club,
buddy. It's great. Okay, certain things are less great
but with Bea (have I told you my better half is
called Bea? Short for Beatrice; she's second generation Dutch) we try to be good parents and friends
to our kids. I also might not have mentioned I have
a daughter, Grace, who is six, but then I started
writing these letters mainly for Cody and kinda
forgot to mention all the members of our little unit.
You'll be a great parent, and, you know, it changes
you, but then you aren't dumb, Lance – you've seen
more of life than your average Joe.

Ha! Average – now that's a word that you'll
never hear describing Lance Armstrong.

Cody says you'll win again next year, and he's an
expert now because he started racing himself. Just
local races, and he's only done a couple, but you
know how it is: the speed, the excitement. Boy, he
loves it. He saved up for that lighter bike I
mentioned last time I wrote, and it's doing him
good. I think he might want to be the next Lance
Armstrong, so you'd better watch out! You never
know – in ten years' time he might be pushing you.

Go Lance – you show them.

God bless, and take care,

Vern, Cody & all the Vurners

The Vurner Family, Biscoe, North Carolina
August 18th, 2000

Dear Lance,

Double Tour of France champion sounds good,
doesn't it? Cody watched every day he could, and
was dancing about and hollering and screaming
when you were showing those pesky Europeans just
who's the boss. It'll do them good to learn how the
Americans do the business.

Cody's racing is progressing nicely; he's going up
state nowadays and most times he comes back with
a real good placing. He's not won yet but it's coming
Lance, it's coming. We try to make it a family affair
when he races: little Grace reads out the list of stuff
we need to load up, Bea gets the drinks and food
prepared and I've been learning how to get Cody's
bike ready. A couple of times I got the wheels the
wrong way round, but he soon sorted me out. I
think it's doing him good to be competing, gaining
confidence and challenging himself. It's good for all
of us being out in the fresh air, building our little
family unit. Cody's schooling has got way better –
no more falling asleep during class. Now he seems
to have more focus on what he's supposed to be
learning and he's still holding down the part-time
job at the hardware store. Can't believe he's stuck
at that as they give him all the carrying and hump-
ing boxes to do. I'm sure he stays at it as it helps

buy more bits for his biking. I said if he gets good
grades this semester then we'll see about getting
him a Trek. I'll have to do a few extra hours at work
but it's for a good cause and he'll be so proud if he
can roll up to his races on a US Postal replica. It
might not be the all singing and dancing carbon one
like you guys, but he'll love it. He already got the
jersey so he'll be a right little Lance.

Just to let you appreciate how much influence
you are having on ordinary folks, I was on the other
side of town and noticed a yard sale. I stopped for a
quick look and I noticed they had a rather dusty old
push bike in the corner. The guy didn't want much
for it and I figured the exercise would be good for
me, so I'm soon to be a born-again cyclist. I haven't
ridden any kind of two wheels since my college days
but once I've sorted out a couple of new tyres, I
reckon I'll be good to go. Bea said I've not to use it
as an excuse to drink more beer.

Do you reckon you'll make it three in a row next
year, Lance? Cody said there's only one other
American who has been that good – some guy from
Minnesota. Or was it Minneapolis? I've never been
good at sport or history, but I know this, Lance:
the things you are doing now with your cancer
foundation and your racing, folks sure are going to
remember your name. Go Lance.

God bless, and take care,

Vern, Cody & all the Vurners

The Vurner Family, Biscoe, North Carolina
December 12th, 2001

Dear Lance,

It's at times like this that the great Americans step
up and are counted, and you, Lance, are one of
those characters we all look up to and respect.
Those guys working at Ground Zero need all the
help they can get, and your taking the time to go
there and show your support meant a lot. President
Bush said what he had to say, but you inspired
those poor guys digging through that mess and
I'm sure they appreciated every moment you were
there and every word you said. Just being from the
same great nation as a guy like you, Lance, makes
me proud. People out there who hate just don't
understand. They aren't educated right and that's
why we're smart and they're wrong. They won't beat
us and they certainly won't beat you, Lance. This
year's French win showed you are too smart and
too strong for the other guys. Three Tours in a row
proves that it's no fluke, that good will out.

On a happier note, I see congratulations are in
order for the arrival of your twins. Boy, you'll be
even busier now they've arrived. Three Tour de
Frances and now three kids. That's proper planning.

I don't know how you do it – fit it all in, I mean.
The hours of training, racing, living overseas and
you still have time to be a great dad and still be

helping the cancer community and inspiring folks. I
guess when you've been through the treatments and
suffering, you know how much it means for someone just to be there, fighting for more to be done.

Our local paper ran a charity bike ride this
summer, just 30 miles round the outskirts of town.
But despite it being a horrible rainy day, we raised
thousands of dollars for some good causes. With
the boys from the bike shop, we laid on some
support for punctures and stuff. I was thinking we
ought to contact your foundation and learn how we
can grow the event and make it a regular thing. I'll
make sure I do that in the new year.

Cody's racing has been a bit hit and miss this
year. First he got sick, then, just as he was coming
strong again, he crashed because some kid slid out
and took half the bunch down. The cuts and bruises
weren't too bad but his beloved new Trek got pretty
chewed up. It's not bent or busted but it ain't the
pretty thing it once was. With exams getting in the
way and him having growing pains, we decided he
ought to take it easy for a while. There was a bit of
trouble afterwards with other parents accusing the
crash-causing kid of being reckless, but we stayed
out of it. I don't want my boy having that attitude
of blaming other folks for things that just happen.

Enjoy your family time and take care. Go Lance.
God bless,
Vern, Cody & all the Vurners

The Vurner Family, Biscoe, North Carolina
June 7th, 2002

Dear Lance,

Best of luck with this year's Tour de France. We'll
be rooting for you as we always have, and we know
you'll be doing America proud by showing the
world that we aren't broken after the events of last
fall. We are all amazed at the impact you've made on
everyone, Lance. Your story really is unique and the
number of people out there being inspired by what
you're doing and how you're doing is just fantastic.

We've been doing our part too in the fight
against cancer and the other folks that need
supporting. Our charity bike ride had 500 more in-
scriptions than the first one so we're hoping that the
money we can collect will be at least doubled. Your
foundation people were a great help in getting us all
organised and everything running safely. Somehow
I've found myself getting more and more involved
even though I'm not really a proper cyclist. Ours is
one of the few families that hasn't been touched by
cancer, but you know I feel just by following you I
ought to be doing something. The town newspaper
guys did some promotions once spring had come
round, and even the local TV station ran a little
story about getting involved. We had lots of
volunteers after that aired – you know, for stuff like
doing the routing and getting drinks stations placed

along the way. I've met so many people I knew from
my school days or work, and it's been great catching
up with them and hearing their stories, even if they
are sometimes with a sad ending.

They all say you've given them hope when they
or those close have been struck down by illness.
And despite it all there are some real jokers amongst
them, I can tell you. I would never have guessed
there were so many cyclists out there, from ordinary
folks just enjoying the freedom, to the guys who
are real experts. Like the two Italian guys who have
come forward to put in some money. They run a
plant hire business on the freeway heading north.
Boy, they know their old cycling stuff. They were
telling Cody and me how they'd been over to the
Champs-Élysées for the last two years and seen you
guys in action. They've got a deal going on with
one of their friends who runs a travel agency in the
mall, so a whole group of them go and have a mini
invasion, meeting up just by the McDonald's.

You've probably seen the Stars and Stripes
waving madly, and heard the American voices
shouting you on. Well, Tony and Steve (they're
fourth-generation immigrants from Milan) are in
amongst that crazy crowd of red, white and blue.
They were saying even though it's a big crowd,
everyone knows the Americans are there.

I don't read the papers much but Cody was
telling me that you are getting some grief from that

guy who used to be our best cyclist, and now he's sore you are more famous and just better than he was. LeMond – jeez, it's even a half-baked French name. He must be one of those guys who wishes he was as popular as you are, Lance. Like the so-called team-mates who left US Postal to try to take you on. Ha!! Fat chance! They ain't got a hope of beating you. Ignore them and keep doing what you're doing. All those famous folks and good people who you know now can't be wrong. Go Lance.

Take care and God bless,

Vern, Cody & all the Vurners

The Vurner Family, Biscoe, North Carolina
November 21st, 2003

Dear Lance,

It doesn't matter what they throw at you, Lance –
you've got them beat at the TdF. I mean, that
Spanish guy, Beloki, falling in front of you, and you
having to go through that field. Man, that was some
quick thinking. It's stuff like that which makes you
the star you are, Lance. Anybody else would have
panicked. I know I would, but you, hey, you had
it all under control. I bet your Hollywood friends'
hearts skipped a few beats with that storyline.
They'll definitely have to put that in the film they
just have to make.

Those celebrities and political folks you've got
coming to see you at races and cancer conventions
are loving being part of such a great movement. I
see your face everywhere – magazines, billboards,
on TV adverts – and I just love when you're on
Letterman. We are all living the Armstrong dream,
and why not? You're unique.

I was kind of hesitant to write about you getting
hooked up with Sheryl Crow, but then I thought
about it, and I guess you deserve some personal
happiness too. You know Bea and I had a rough
patch in our marriage at the beginning, and it was
touch and go for a while, but then Cody came along
and things got better slowly. I guess I just stepped

up, but I've got friends who weren't so lucky and they split up, so I guess Kristin and you couldn't work it out. I'm sorry that was how it turned out. It can't have been easy with you gone so much, but I know you'll still be a good parent because you're a great guy and wouldn't want to set a bad example to your kids.

Damn, Lance, Sheryl Crow is hot, so it's kinda worked out for you again. I mean, who would have thought you'd be bringing all those famous folks out in support of cancer and learning how great cycling is? You're making the sport global, Lance, and none of those other guys who won five Tour de Frances get anywhere near that fame. I don't doubt you'll be moving ahead of them next year.

Tony and Steve sponsored our Livestrong bike ride with even more money this year and the weather was great. The crowds came out and we've started a kids ride too. You have to get them hooked young, don't you?

We've just been watching the video of their Tour visit and, boy, it was something. They did the last ten days but I don't know if you spotted them. I guess not as there was just so many folks from the USA there rooting for you each day. I said to Cody afterwards we need to go next year and see the Tour for ourselves. He'll be off to college in 2006 but be back home for the summer break so we can fit it in.

His racing has kinda got stuck at state level, as

he just doesn't have the time, and with him off to California studying, I guess it'll be on hold even more then. He's got a scholarship offer from one of the guys, Wayne, who I met whilst doing our Livestrong ride. Poor guy's wife died from stomach cancer last winter. So he runs this video games company and they have a deal out in Santa Monica to train young guys. We got talking and he offered Cody a deal to get through college and a job later. Since those computer games are Cody's other passion, it's a great opportunity for him.

I was stepped up to management level at work three months ago, so I reckon what with more money coming in and not having to do emergency call-outs at weekends, I'll have more time to get some cycling done. We've done the sums, and we can save enough to do a trip to Europe next year, so hopefully we'll see you there. Go Lance.

God bless, and take care,

Vern, Cody & all the Vurners

The Vurner Family, Biscoe, North Carolina
July 31st, 2004

Dear Lance,

Well, we made it to Paris, and what an experience! I didn't realise just how big of an event the Tour is. I mean, I've seen it on TV, and the videos that Tony and Steve made, but, damn, it's huge. It's crazy. And seeing you in yellow behind all the US Postal guys leading the race through the finish was just fantastic. We had our flag waving and Cody hollered so much he couldn't speak afterwards. What an honour to see you make history, Lance. Six Tours in a row! First guy to do that – unbelievable.

I can see why the guys in our group get out there each year and be part of it all. I wish we had done the last week from the mountains, but what with the Amsterdam visit to Bea's long-lost relatives and the limited time I had on vacation from work, we just couldn't fit it all in. Maybe next year.

We met up with the other guys from Biscoe – Tony and Steve, Wayne and his wife Liz and the guy who sets it all up, Mike, and his wife Susie. Funny thing is, I'd done an air-con installation at Mike's house and didn't realise it was his place, only having dealt with Susie there. It was a big surprise to learn our wives knew each other from their high-school days and us guys had seen each other on the Livestrong rides. I never knew he lived up on the hill in the big houses. I guess the travel business pays well. I think Bea and Susie are planning on keeping in touch more now they know their men are out riding together. It's strange how cycling brings folks together.

Cody's first term at college is going well. He took his Trek with him to campus, but he says he's not had time to do much riding, though he did say they have local races and he might try out the competition once he's training again. I think he's being optimistic trying to fit in everything now that he's discovered partying and girls. We know how much attention they take up, don't we?

I saw Sheryl Crow up in the tribunes by the finish line. Wow, buddy – she's lookin' good.

You know, Lance, I've been thinking about how good our lives have been since that day Cody came home with his sports project and he spoke about you. We've learned so much about you and our-selves in just following your story, it's been amazing. All the people round about you, the cancer commu-nity and the sport of cycling, have just got bigger and stronger. Even the French are beginning to realise they need you, Lance. Holy crap – you have presidents and rock stars using you to look cool, and yet they still try to put you down. You're bigger than them all and a great American. Go Lance.

God bless, and take care,

Vern, Cody & all the Vurners

The Vurner Family, Biscoe, North Carolina
August 1st, 2005

Dear Lance,

It was one of the best moments of my life, Lance, to be there in Paris and witness you stand on that Tour de France podium and give your final winner's speech with your kids by your side.

Folks everywhere ought to listen to what you said and respect your example of humility and honest, hard work. Livestrong bands everywhere, America standing proud behind you – boy, that was good to be part of. I don't see why you are stopping now you've got seven wins. You could have eight or nine. The other guys like Ulrich and Basso aren't even close. But, you know, I've learned to respect what you've been doing and saying, and so if you decide you want to stop racing, then you go for it.

You can do anything you want, Lance. I read the jealous people saying stuff that you ain't smart enough to be a politician, but why not run for Governor? It's not as if you don't have the connections. And don't forget ordinary people believe in what you stand for. I know you've been hanging out with President Bush, and though I didn't vote for the Republicans, I'd sure back you if I was a Texan. It's not the politics I care about – it's the guy's beliefs that count.

All that crap about you having to do drugs and

cheating is just baloney. Those guys who don't get it
are just sore losers. You've looked death in the face
and have come back. You don't need to cheat to
prove nothing, Lance. You've got a great life, great
kids and a good woman beside you – that's why they
are jealous. Shit, even the guys who left your team
and tried to beat you, like Hamilton, never could,
despite you teaching them how much work they had
to do. Even on drugs, they still aren't good enough.
Thankfully, some of the new Americans coming
through are following your example – good hard
work and an honest-to-God spirit. Yeah, I know you
aren't that religious but you have that spirit, Lance.

Cody's back racing a bit – just college races
– but enough to stop him going the wrong way.
He's hooked up with a Spanish girl so I'm kinda
hoping he'll settle down and graduate with some
good grades. Little Grace ain't little any more. She's
in high school now and, to tell the truth, has been
struggling a bit. I think she misses her big brother
and, you know, being a teenager is tough these days.
I guess you're going have to go through similar
stuff with your kids. We all do.

Bea's went back to work part-time, in Mike's
travel business, and she's been going to the gym
with Susie two days a week. I've found coming
home to an empty home a bit strange on those days
but she's loving the freedom of the kids growing up
and becoming more independent.

Our Livestrong ride is well established now. The committee meetings are less like a business meeting and more like a group of buddies hanging out. Tony and Steve are still sponsoring most of it, and despite being wiped out by some jerk in an SUV, they are out riding most weekends. They were shook up pretty bad by the accident, but they're okay now.

You know, Lance, now you have more time on your hands, maybe we could have you up here cutting the ribbon for our ride. Ha!! You never know, maybe one day. Go Lance.

God bless, and take care,

Vern, Cody & all the Vurners

The Vurner Family, Biscoe, North Carolina
January 26th, 2007

Dear Lance,

I can see you're enjoying your new retired life, and
why not? Now that you're single again, you can play
the field again – show Sheryl she missed out. That
was quite a thing to run the New York marathon in
under three hours. I know a couple of guys who do
a serious bit of running, and they were saying they'd
struggle to get near that, so how you managed that,
what with all the work you put in for Livestrong and
your travelling with your celebrity friends, I don't
know. I guess when you have your physical gifts you
can put your hand to most things.

   You're best out of the European cycling scene,
what with all that Operation Puerto business going
on. Jeez, I thought the Spanish were a relaxed
lot but it looks like they've been at the centre of
some pretty bad drugs. Thing is, some folks are so
desperate to be successful that they'll do anything.
You know, it's like those legal jerks and former team
members you have to keep fighting off, looking to
bring you down or avoid paying out what you're
due. It beggars belief how low some folks will
stoop. I'd have hoped just being part of your team
at US Postal was enough, but it seems not.

   Don't get me started on the French newspapers
or I'll get real angry. Losers the lot of them. Then

there's guys like Landis getting pinged at the Tour.
I know that's not something he'd have learned with
you at US Postal. I guess his lack of morals is why
he thought he could get away with cheating and why
he chose a foreign team for that. Maybe that Amish
stuff ain't all it's cracked up to be. It ain't normal
still using horses and carts for your transport or not
drinking a good cold beer now and then.

Cody's settled in over in California. His cycling
has taken a back seat while he studies but I know
he'll be back at it once he graduates. Real big news
here is I'm going to be a grandpa in a couple of
months thanks to him and his girlfriend Marie. I
was kinda hoping they'd get married beforehand but
it's not happening. They both said it's not the
modern way so I guess we'll just have to go with
what they want. Bea was a bit put out at first, but
she's come over to the idea now. Hey, it's not like
she's got much choice now, is it?

At work I'm a proper manager now, looking
after commercial installations and some contract-
ing. We've diversified into sanitation too. You
know that's something I noticed when I was over
in France – their standards aren't what we are used
to. I wouldn't say they were dirty but we're used to
better wash-rooms than they think are okay. Maybe
you just got used to it but that was something that
bugged me.

Now I do nine till five and the odd conference

weekend, which means plenty of time for riding after work with my buddies. We've got a good little group together that meets up twice a week by the new bike shop that's opened in town.

We hammer it for a couple of hours and then grab a beer afterwards, and, you know, I must be getting pretty fit as I can hold my own with most of them. Sure, our Italian duo of Tony and Steve kick my butt but I can still keep up with Mike, and he's nearly ten years younger than me. It must be the Lance effect. Bea and Susie have become real good friends so if I come home from work and she's not in, I know she'll be round their house. In case you were wondering how Grace is doing, don't ask. She's okay with being an aunt as long as she can still be an Emo. Yeah, I don't know what that is either. Go Lance.

God bless, and take care,

Vern, Cody & all the Vurners

The Vurner Family, Biscoe, North Carolina
May 19th, 2009

Dear Lance,

I couldn't believe it when I read you were making a comeback. You know, I thought for a moment you were slightly crazy. Then I realised you're Lance Armstrong! You know what you're doing. You've seen the new guys and noticed they ain't all that.

Even stuff like getting busted up at Gila won't stop you from being at the Tour for another win. It's a pity your people couldn't find some backing in the States but I'm sure you'll sort out those Astana folks real quick. With your guys in there, everything will be organised as you like it. It'll shut up all the sceptics once you show them you have nothing to hide. They can test you all they like but we know you're clean. As you say, the most tested athlete on the planet. You should add 'and the greatest'.

So do you think you'll settle down with this new girl, Anna? I guess it's serious if you guys have a baby on the way. You know, she seems a good choice for you: grounded, sensible. All that razzamatazz with the red carpet people and hanging with guys like Bono isn't the real world, and one thing I've always admired about you, Lance, is you've stayed close to real people. Look at what you do with Livestrong – out there, pushing for more to be done. Okay, I understand that US politics ain't your thing now but you're still there pushing for hospitals and research, still campaigning for good things to be done. That's a proper legacy right there.

Cody graduated and is working out in California for Wayne. He's doing video games designs and future projects, apparently. He's got a good life out there with Marie and little Max. We visited not long back and went for a bike ride together. Just like the old days, it was, and he can still kick my ass.

Our Biscoe Livestrong day is as popular as ever: couple of thousand last year and already that many signed for next month's ride. All the local businesses are involved now, from the hotels and bike shops through to the burger places and taxis, they are all saying they love Fight Cancer week. I'm proud I'm involved and showing that cycling can improve ordinary folks' health. I was down in Austin a few months ago for a seminar and stopped off at your Mellow Johnny's on the drive back. Nice place you got there. I bought Cody and Grace a T-shirt each and almost got myself a SRAM groupset. Boy, I was tempted but then I thought if you're doing the Tour again I could use the money for another Paris trip. Maybe not this year as I can't change my vacation dates so you'll have to continue racing in 2010. Bea said we can go but only if we do all the proper tourist stuff this time. Go Lance.

God bless, and take care,

Vern, Cody & all the Vurners

The Vurner Family, Biscoe, North Carolina
February 6th, 2010

Dear Lance,

How you doing? I can't believe the Feds are still
chasing you. Some of the guys were saying it's all
a political conspiracy. You know, what with you
being friends with President Bush and then thinking
about running for office yourself. That probably
upset the Establishment that someone like you
could be more powerful than they are. I don't get
why the Government is wasting our money on crap
like this when they could be backing Livestrong's
goals or getting fat kids doing some exercise.

You just keep your head down, Lance. This
will all blow over, and don't let it affect your racing
or your foundation. You could have won a couple
more Tours without this crap hanging over you.

I don't see why there's so many angry people out
there. Don't they see the good you've done? Sure,
you don't get to the top without some folks getting
pushed out the way – that's life – but look at what
you've done for cycling, for the cancer community.
They'd still be stuck at the bottom of the mountain
wishing they had someone to show them the way.

I see that loser Landis is still around too. Oh
Lord, he needs to man up and accept it's his own
fault he messed up and now no one wants him on a
bike team.

You probably guessed it but we didn't make last year's Tour. Cody and Marie's beautiful little Max had a health scare so we stayed at home. The doctors thought he had meningitis but thankfully after a heap of tests it was just some rare virus, so he's alright now. You know it's at times like that you need family and good friends around. Stay strong Lance.

God bless, and take care,

Vern, Cody & all the Vurners

The Vurner Family, Biscoe, North Carolina
August 23rd, 2010

Dear Lance,

Well, you tried for your best for one last Tour and time finally caught up with you. But you know what, Lance? It's not always the result that counts; sometimes the journey there is just as important. Yeah, I know you're a winner and it sucks not winning another Tour, but look at how many people were inspired by you. Even those grumpy Frenchies saw they needed your presence to bring in the crowds. They'll struggle without you, Lance. We all will.

We were glad we could see your final Tour for ourselves. That's right – we made it to Paris kinda thanks to a deal I put together for the company. I was in the process of putting together the tenders for an installation we were doing out of town when Tony mentioned he knew a guy, Italian of course, who might want to help out. So they got in touch and flew me out to Milan to their factory and we eventually agreed on a deal. Good thing is, Tony's friend, Emilio, is into cycling too so we probably talked more about that than we did about anything work related. You know, he even invited me to join them on L'Etape du Tour – the amateur ride over the Tour mountains. The factory have a corporate day there. Didn't even cost me anything and they loaned me a Colnago bike when I said I was

travelling with the family and we didn't have the
space. Saved me no end of money on excess, that
did, so what with them paying my trip to France, I
had enough to bring Grace along with me and Bea.
Tony and Steve came too, of course.

I guess you know how hard those mountains
are. Boy, I suffered. It was the same route you guys
did for stage 19. The Col du Telegraphe was enough
for me and even after stopping at a feed station for
15 minutes I was in real trouble trying to get up the
Galibier. I don't know how you guys do it, I really
don't. I had to stop when I started getting cramps
five miles from the top. If it hadn't been for good
old Tony staying with me and then giving me some
aspirins he had to help me out, I would have just
fallen asleep there and then. You know what, I'm
glad he did because I perked up after that stop and
drank plenty of water on the long descent to that
real pretty lake.

By the time I reached the bottom of Alpe
d'Huez we were flying, passing guys like they were
standing still. Tony kept telling me to slow down, to
save something for the climb but I was feeling so
good I ignored him and pressed on. Of course, two
corners in and I blew big time. I think it was just
where you left Ulrich back in 2001. You might not
realise it but it's a long way from there to the top
when you're not in good shape, but I'm glad I did it.

I know we take more than twice as long as you

guys but that's okay – we can dream. Funny thing was, even though I was worn out, I couldn't sleep that night. Tony said it was probably the excitement of just being there, doing what you guys do. I guess he's right, but, you know, doing those 106 kilometres was awesome and I now know I need something like the Colnago they loaned me. Maybe I'll come past Mellow Johnny's and see what deal you can put together on one of those carbon beauties that Trek have out this year. Cody will be so jealous.

Bea and Grace didn't want to see the last stage on the Champs Elysees as they said it was boring so they went off to do the Eiffel Tower and the other tourist traps while we got our Big Macs and joined the American mob outside the big M. It was just as mad as the other times I'd been and just as good. You guys put on a great show.

So now I'm back at the daily grind and wondering what you're going to do next, Lance. One thing's for sure: it'll be special. Go Lance.

God bless, and take care,

Vern & all the Vurners

The Vurner Family, Biscoe, North Carolina
February 15th, 2013

Dear Lance,

I watched and hoped, read the stories where they
slated you, and all those old team-mates accused
you of everything under the sun. I watched the
Feds investigate you and find nothing, even though
the end of that smelled bad. Did you call in some
favours or something? It wouldn't surprise me now.
I still believed in you, Lance. I believed because the
Feds walked away, and they don't do that, ever. So
then there were only the guys I thought were the
sad losers left. Picking at you and what you've done
because they weren't as good and had their own
interests to push. But what do I believe now?

I used to say USADA and all those other sports
organisations needed to back off, but after the
Oprah interview I can see that you are one messed-
up individual. The drugs, the bullying, the intimida-
tion – it's all true. You said it was all true. Damn!!!

I don't know why I even started with Dear
Lance. I guess I, at least, still have some standards.
It's more than I can say for your sorry ass.

Look at your so-called friends since you sat on
Oprah's sofa and told your version of the truth: the
Nikes, Oakleys, Treks, they're all leaving you now.
They don't want you now, do they? You might learn

what it's like to feel used now you are soiled goods.
I thought for a moment you might even shed a few
tears for Oprah. That would have been even better
for her ratings. Oh boy, now we all know what an
ugly person you've been. Was that the real truth,
Lance? Was that all of it or have you kept some
back because your legal guys told you to? I guess
you'll have them on speed dial from now on.

What are we supposed to do for Livestrong day
here in Biscoe? Cover over your photos, for sure.
We don't want the smell that's stuck to you now. It's
supposed to be healthy and nice but you ain't been
that for a long time. What about the foundation?
You need to apologize to all the good folks there,
really apologize, not just do a TV spot. The Hollywood and White House visits are over, Lance.

I phoned Cody straight after the interview and
he wasn't surprised. He said I needed to open my
eyes to the shit in the world around me. I asked
what he meant, and he said I'd become obsessed
with cycling, and even more so with you. I thought
I was getting closer to him but he said he'd given up
on you long ago. He was only keeping me happy.
Bea just shrugged her shoulders and so did the guys
I ride with. Damn, I feel like a fool. You aren't a
great American at all – you're a fraud. I feel sorry
for your family and kids, but not for you. Not at all.

V V

Vernon Vurner, Troy, North Carolina
July 12th, 2013

Dear Lance,

I hope you noticed the address above. I ain't living
in Biscoe no more and I ain't playing happy families
either. I did want to blame you, Lance, but I guess
like Cody said, I'd become obsessed and stopped
being a proper husband and proper dad. Bea has
been cheating on me with that two-faced ass Mike
for the last six years and I didn't notice nothing was
up. Worse still, Cody has known for a while but
didn't dare tell me. At least Grace was spared the
hurt until we split up.

Your Oprah confession was the start of the
end for us. Bea changed – going out, staying out. I
thought it was me being depressed that made her
stay away but it was more than that.

Then I discovered the truth one afternoon.
I'd finished early at work because a meeting fell
through so I headed home and thought I'd surprise
Bea with an afternoon out in the park. But she
wasn't home, so I got my cycling gear on and,
assuming she was at the gym with Susie, I went
down there. They weren't, and her cellphone was
off so I headed up to Susie's house thinking they
would be there, and, sure enough, there was her
car outside. Then I heard laughing from the back
yard and, since I usually left my Trek round by the

pool-house when I popped past, I went through the side gate and was just about to put my bike against the fence when I heard more noise. Different noises this time. So I sneaked up to the window of the pool-house and there she was. With Mike. He had a US Postal jersey on and there he was banging my Bea, and she was laughing and giggling and saying to him, 'Go Lance, Go Lance, give me some of your magic potion.'

They thought it was funny – oh so funny. I didn't know what to do as they hadn't seen or heard me, so I got on my bike and went home. And waited for her. When she came back, she didn't deny it, wasn't sorry neither. Apparently I was useless and a nerd. Mike was the man for her and the last straw was when I started shaving my legs for the Livestrong day. She's been banging Mike on and off for six years, and I didn't notice. What a fool.

I tried – I really tried to fix us – but it wasn't the same. Bea wasn't interested, so two months ago I moved out and we've started the divorce. Susie has left Mike and went to live with her sister down Florida way. Wayne let me stay in his RV while I sorted out somewhere new, and now I'm holed up in a condo in Troy. Our old house has just sold after taking an offer way below what it's worth, but I ain't arguing – I just want it finished. Grace has cried most nights but Cody's okay. Well, he says he is.

I'm having a break from the cycling whilst I
sort myself out. They can do the Livestrong charity
stuff without me. I need a rest from all the crap of
the Lance Armstrong story and the cheating you
brought to my life. Just like you ended up with
Discovery, I've ended up with my own discovery.
And you know what ? Both stink.

Vernon Vurner, Troy, North Carolina
December 2nd, 2013

Dear Lance,

I don't know if I can forgive you for what you've done. I certainly won't forget what has happened to my family and the people I've come to know through Livestrong. I used to ignore all those sad people who said you were a cheat, a liar, a fraud, and now I'm the fool. I don't know what will happen to you now, Lance. I don't know if I should care or not. I feel sorry for your wife and your kids and how you've hurt all those people from the cancer community who trusted you. But Lance Armstrong the so-called hero is over for me. So I'm on my own now, but you know what? I can look myself in the face and not be ashamed.

I'll go out riding with my real buddies and, though I'll never be rich or famous, I can sleep easy at night. And I can go racing if I want.

Bye Lance.

Robert Millar is a former professional cyclist who finished fourth in the 1984 Tour de France – then the best result by a British rider – and won the king of the mountains jersey. Now he writes for *Rouleur* and cyclingnews.com

4

Ernest Hemingway never produced a book solely about cycling – at least, not one that was ever published.

But, **Brendan Gallagher** discovers, bike racing peppers many of his other works, demonstrating just how much 'Papa' loved the sport.

CYCLING AND HEMINGWAY

BY BRENDAN GALLAGHER

Ernest Hemingway lost manuscripts all over France in the 1920s, but, alas, it seems an in-depth appreciation of cycling doesn't appear to have been among them. His first wife Hadley famously mislaid just about everything her husband had written in the early Paris years, bar two short stories he had sent to prospective publishers, when leaving a bag unattended at the Gare de Lyon one morning as she travelled to join him in Geneva. Nothing was ever recovered. Meanwhile, much later in his life, the concierge at the Ritz in Paris suddenly remembered an entire tea chest of abandoned notebooks and half-finished stories he had left there 20 years earlier and they subsequently formed the basis of *A Moveable Feast*.

Would it be too much to ask that somewhere at his old haunts – The Gritti Palace hotel and Harry's Bar in Venice, The Dorchester in London, the Hotel Florida in Madrid, the La Consula Residence in Malaga or one of his favourite hotels and watering holes in Havana and New York – there is another

long-forgotten tea chest or travel bag buried under a
mountain of dust?

For years I could never go into the large waiting
room at the old Reading railway station – the one on
the left next to The Three Guineas pub by the main
London line – without the thought that many years
earlier T E Lawrence had left the original, just completed, manuscript of *Seven Pillars of Wisdom* there
one panicky afternoon. I could never resist a quick
glance around, just in case. It was never found, and
Lawrence had to start again from scratch, although
he was unhappy with the resulting 'classic'. Just think
how good the original might have been. Did it end
up in a dustbin, or is it still out there somewhere?

We can dream, but Hemingway on cycling is,
alas, the masterpiece we have to realistically accept
never got written despite his fascination with the
sport and its associated milieu for much of the
1920s when he lived in Paris and roamed extensively
throughout France, Italy and Spain.

For a while, at least, cycling seemed to offer up
everything he loved in sport and life: men *in extre-
mis*, rugged topography and weather, grace under
pressure, messianic devotion to an almost religious
higher cause, suffering for the common good, an
enclosed, self-perpetuating 'in-crowd'. But there
was also the cheating born of economic necessity,
the cunning of low people in high places, the dodgy
promoters and team managers, and the greedy pilot

fish feeding off the peloton. It was a man's world
– which Hemingway loved – but women, strangely
drawn to the conquering heroes, also seemed attract-
ed to the sport and its gladiators, and that fascinated
him as well.

It was all there for Hemingway: the heat and
clamour, the high mountain passes, big skies, the
rain and fog, back-of-the-hand conversations before
and after races. And of course the intricate tactics
and techniques which needed to be understood and
mastered before he would attempt to explain them to
a wider public in other sporting arenas. Manna from
heaven for the literary alpha male, surely?

So, why no cycling book? There are tantalising
scraps on the subject littered throughout his various
novels, correspondence and the memoirs of others
– much more of which anon – and indeed evidence
that on more than one occasion he sat down with
the specific intention of trying to do cycling justice.
Yet in his 20s, by his own admission, this apparently
fearless writer on just about every physical activity
under the sun seemed to recoil from such a seemingly simple and enjoyable task.

During those Paris years, Hemingway was busy
trying to make ends meet through numerous journalistic assignments for the *Toronto Star* – payment
was by the article and indeed by the word – and also
trying to perfect an individualistic and revolutionary
style to novel-writing, as witnessed in *The Sun Also*

Rises and *A Farewell to Arms*. With time and money in relatively short supply – at least in his own mind, although both his wives of their era had inherited considerable dowries – he was in no mood to be derailed by the indulgent luxury of a 'cycling book', which might or might not sell. Frustratingly, however, cycling features in both of those early novels mentioned, either directly or subliminally.

There was also the distracting and energy-consuming matter of becoming a father, embarking on a nerve-shredding affair with Pauline Pfeiffer, divorcing Hadley, marrying Pfeiffer and then moving back to America and the sleepy backwaters of the Florida Keys, which was the death knell as far as a cycling book was concerned. Out of sight, out of mind.

In his literary maturity, he was far too engaged on other projects: big-game fishing, African safaris, war in all its forms, and the perennial battle of the sexes. And, finally, as Hemingway hurtled towards a premature death by his own hand, the words began to fail him altogether, and it was too late.

Just before that suicidal nadir, however, he enjoyed a literary Indian summer, and penned his last wholly satisfying book, *A Moveable Feast*, when, in the way that old men invariably review and revise their halcyon youth, he revisited the Paris years – a journey that occasionally takes in his love of cycling. It was the discovery of that tea chest full of memories and scribbled notes at the Ritz that kickstarted the whole process.

At one point in *A Moveable Feast*, when discussing the suggestion of his good friend Mike Ward – best man at his second marriage – that he should wean himself off the ruinous business of horse racing and trying to beat the bookies, Hemingway starts writing unexpectedly about cycling and in particular the *Six Jours* – Six-Day racing – in Paris. The passage lacks a good deal of punctuation – full-stops or semi-colons are as rare as hens' teeth – and, with the occasional word seemingly omitted, it has the feel of extended notes made live at the velodrome, with the intention of possibly working them up into some-thing more substantial at a future date.

In the event, he decided to reproduce them unedited in a chapter entitled *The End of an Avocation*.

'I have started many stories about bicycle racing but have never written one that is as good as the races are both on the indoor and outdoor tracks and on the roads,' he admits, candidly, before it all starts gushing out in a stream of consciousness as he outlines the story he wishes he was able to pen.

'But I will get to the Vélodrome d'Hiver with the smoky light of the afternoon and the high-banked wooden track and the whirring sound the tires made on the wood as the riders passed, the effort and the tactics as the riders climbed and plunged, each one a part of his machine; I will get the magic of the *demi-fond*, the noise of the motors with their rollers set out behind them that the *entraîneurs* rode, wearing their heavy crash helmets and leaning backward in their ponderous leather suits, to shelter the riders who followed them from the air resistance, the riders in their lighter crash helmets bent low over their handlebars their legs turning the huge gear sprockets and the small front wheels touching the roller behind the machine that gave them the shelter to ride in, and the duels that were more exciting than anything, the *put-puting* of the motorcycles and the riders elbow to elbow and wheel to wheel up and down and around at deadly speed until one man could not hold the pace and broke away and the solid wall of air that he had been sheltered against hit him.

'There were so many kinds of racing. The straight sprints raced in heats or in match races where the two riders would balance for long seconds on their machines for the advantage of making the other rider take the lead and then the slow circling and the final plunge into the driving purity of speed. There were the programs of the team races of two hours, with a series of pure sprints in their heats to fill the afternoon, the lonely absolute speed events of one man racing an hour against the clock, the terribly dangerous and beautiful races of one hundred kilometers on the big banked wooden five-hundred-meter bowl of the Stade Buffalo, the outdoor stadium of Montrouge where they raced behind big motorcycles, Linart, the great Belgian champion that they called "the Sioux" for his profile, dropping his head to suck up cherry brandy from a rubber tube that connected with a hot water bottle under his racing shirt when he needed it toward the end as he increased his savage speed. And the championships of France behind the big motors of the six-hundred-and-sixty-meter cement track of the Parc du Prince near Auteuil, the wickedest track of all where we saw the great rider Ganay fall and heard his skull crumple under the crash helmet as you crack a hardboiled egg against a stone to peel it on a picnic. I must write the strange world of the six-day races and the marvels of the road-racing in the mountains. French is the only language it has ever been written in properly and the terms are all French and that is what makes it hard to write.'

* * *

There is no doubt that Hemingway was, for a time, a genuine and enthusiastic follower of the Six-Day events at the three major velodromes in Paris. On two documented occasions – in 1927 with his new wife, Pauline, and in 1929 with his good friend and drinking partner Guy Hickock – he also travelled to Berlin specifically to watch the Six-Day races, which was no small or cheap undertaking. He was a fan as well as an observer.

It seems clear, unless he was taking massive liberties with the truth, that he witnessed first-hand the tragic death of Gustave Ganay at the Parc des Princes on August 23, 1926, while the Victor Linart he mentions in *A Moveable Feast* was a permanent fixture at the Six-Day meets of the day. The tough and durable Belgian rider won the world professional motor-paced championships on four occasions between 1920 and 1931, including the 1924 championships in Paris (which Hemingway possibly witnessed), and made a handsome living riding the circuit. He was nicknamed 'the Sioux' on account of his dark skin colour and a badly flattened nose – the result of a nasty accident when he crashed at high speed in 1912.

The world of Six-Day racing ticked a lot of boxes for Hemingway. Again, an apparently open and unambiguous sporting spectacle, it was in fact more akin to a 'show' – a production that was in fact run by an in-crowd with their own rules and hierarchy, something which continued into modern times. If you were a member of the so-called 'Blue Train', you were guaranteed rides and regular income through the long winter months, but, if you existed outside of it, life was much more precarious.

With abundant energy to burn, Hemingway also enjoyed the extraordinary racing hours, with the action often continuing until dawn, which provided a ready excuse to get up and about eating and drinking in the small hours. Ad-hoc night clubs and cafes were constructed overnight at the velodromes, and there was a fascinating social scene to be observed and enjoyed. After Hadley grew tired of the late nights, disappearing to the *Six Jours* offered up a heaven-sent opportunity to quietly court Pauline without his advances being too obvious in the generally chaotic party-going scene.

Hemingway also found the highly charged atmosphere extremely energising and creative, especially when attending on his own when he was able to settle into a rhythm. In the centre of the velodrome, where the journalists would be roped off and herded into a media area, he proofread and reworked *The Torrents of Spring* and *A Farewell to Arms*, and worked extensively on the galley proofs of *The Sun Also Rises*, which to the non-writer might seem extraordinary.

However, as even the most humble journalist will tell you – and Hemingway started life as precisely that – there are two optimum working conditions when you are writing or finalising a piece. You either need the cathedral-like silence of your office or attic – with the family banished to the living room or, better still, sent to play in the park or despatched to visit relatives – or the womb-like comfort of a busy press centre at a big event, where every single noise and voice miraculously disappears, consumed by the general hum and hubbub, a constant and reassuring heartbeat on which you can thrive. It is much easier to concentrate when 6,000 fans are screeching at the top of their voices and a gaggle of 20 or so journalists are laughing and joking than when you are working alone and one lone voice is talking in the room next door or the couple next door are having an argument.

Bored of his attic-room existence and/or the infant shouts of his young son Bumby, Hemingway found the middle of the Vélodrome d'Hiver, the Parc des Princes, and occasionally the Stade Buffalo, extremely congenial and efficient places to work.

A taste of Hemingway flourishing in these improvised offices comes in *Papa Hemingway* – a personal memoir written by his most eloquent and admiring Boswell, AE Hotchner, who recalls scores of conversations and letters over the decades on a wide range of subjects. In the chapter 'Paris, 1950', he quotes Hemingway recalling his halcyon days in the capital: 'I'll never forget the time I set up operations in a box at the finish line of the six-day bike races, to work on the proofs of *A Farewell to Arms*. There was good inexpensive champagne and when I got hungry they sent over Crabe Mexicaine from Prunier. I had rewritten the ending thirty-nine times in manuscript and now I worked it over thirty times in proof, trying to get it right. I finally got it right.'

In the same chapter, Hemingway also explained how he started writing *A Farewell to Arms* at the Vélodrome d'Hiver after a nasty accident the previous day when the skylight in the toilet at the Closerie de Lilas cafe crashed on his head causing a gaping head wound. Somehow the blood and gore seemed to galvanise him: 'The next day I went to the bike races and that evening, feeling absolutely wonderful from the loss of all that blood, I finally began to write *A Farewell to Arms*.'

* * *

Around that time – 1927 – and with his head full of cycling, Hemingway published 'A Pursuit Race' in his collection of short stories, entitled *Men Without Women*. Alas, for cycling fans, he uses cycling only as a metaphor for the chaotic relationship being played out between William Campbell – a drunken, drug-taking and highly stressed advance man for a burlesque show – and Mr Turner, the show's owner and Campbell's boss. Turner catches up with Campbell in Kansas City, finds him in a terribly debauched state, and fires him, albeit reluctantly because in many ways he sympathises with his employee. Campbell is replaced by the Nick Adams character – a regular in Hemingway's short stories, and somewhat of an alter ego.

At the start, Hemingway writes: 'William Campbell had been in a pursuit race with a burlesque show ever since Pittsburgh. In a pursuit race, in bicycle racing, riders start at equal intervals to ride after one another. They ride very fast because the race is usually limited to a short distance and if they slow their riding another rider who maintains his pace will make up the space that separated them equally at the start. As soon as the rider is caught and passed he is out of the race and must get down from his bicycle and leave the track. If none of the riders are caught the winner of the race is the one who has gained the most distance. In most pursuit races, if there are only two riders, one of the riders is caught inside of six miles. The burlesque show caught William Campbell at Kansas City.'

The metaphor doesn't altogether work, and Hemingway made no great claims for the story, but that chilling line, 'As soon as the rider is caught and passed he is out of the race and must get down from his bicycle and leave the track,' is a pretty decent summing-up of his uncompromising approach to life. The message is clear enough.

Throughout this period, Hemingway also followed the road cycling scene. *The Sun Also Rises* – his first major commercial success – includes quite a lengthy passage in which another alter ego, Jake Barnes, takes time out from the incessant partying and romantic intrigue of his dysfunctional gang's visit to the *corrida* at Pamplona to escape to San Sebastian for a few days, where he observes the arrival and departure of the Tour du Pays Basque – the Tour of the Basque Country stage race. It's a fascinating and ambiguous passage, and can be read on two levels. Firstly, from that of a sports-minded journalist automatically recording and assessing what he sees. And secondly, while doing that, he instantly realises that there is some distance between what the public are allowed to see and the reality of what is occurring. He immediately latches on to another in-crowd with their own coded messages and close-knit way of life, but you can sense an envy at the collec-tive esprit of the peloton, which is in stark contrast to the warring friends he had just left in Pamplona.

'Later when it began to get dark, I walked around the harbor and out along the promenade, and finally back to the hotel for supper. There was a bicycle-race on, the Tour du Pays Basque, and the riders were stopping that night in San Sebastian. In the dining-room, at one side, there was a long table of bicycle-riders, eating with their trainers and managers. They were all French and Belgians, and paid close attention to their meal, but they were having a good time. At the head of the table were two good-looking French girls, with much Rue du Faubourg Montmartre chic. I could not make out whom they belonged to. They all spoke in slang at the long table and there were many private jokes and some jokes at the far end that were not repeated when the girls asked to hear them. The next morning at five o'clock the race resumed with the last lap, San Sebastian-Bilbao. The bicycle-riders drank much wine, and were burned and browned by the sun. They did not take the race seriously except among themselves. They had raced among themselves so often that it did not make much difference who won. Especially in a foreign country. The money could be arranged.

'The man who had a matter of two minutes lead in the race had an attack of boils, which were very painful. He sat on the small of his back. His neck was very red and the blond hairs were sunburned. The other riders joked him about his boils. He tapped on the table with his fork. "Listen," he said, "to-morrow my nose is so tight on the handlebars that the only thing touches those boils is a lovely breeze."

'One of the girls looked at him down the table, and he grinned and turned red. The Spaniards, they said, did not know how to pedal.

'I had coffee out on the *terrasse* with the team manager of one of the big bicycle manufacturers. He said it had been a very pleasant race, and would have been worth watching if Bottechia [sic] had not abandoned it at Pamplona. The dust had been bad, but in Spain the roads were better than in France. Bicycle road-racing was the only sport in the world, he said. Had I ever followed the Tour de France? Only in the papers. The Tour de France was the greatest sporting event in the world. Following and organizing the road races had made him know France. Few people know France. All spring and all summer and all fall he spent on the road with bicycle road-racers. Look at the number of motor-cars now that followed the riders from town to town in a road race. It was a rich country and more *sportif* every year. It would be the most *sportif* country in the world. It was bicycle road-racing that did it. That and football. He knew France. *La France Sportive*. He knew road-racing. We had a cognac. After all, though, it wasn't bad to get back to Paris. There is only one Paname. In all the world, that is. Paris is the town the most *sportif* in the world. Did I know the Chope de Negre? Did I not. I would see him there some time. I certainly would. We would drink another fine together. We certainly would. They started at six o'clock less a quarter in the morning. Would I be up for the *depart*? I would certainly try to. Would I like him to call me? It was very interesting. I would leave a call at the desk. He would not mind calling me. I could not let him take the trouble. I would leave a call at the desk. We said good-bye until the next morning.'

Searching through the early records of the Tour du Pays Basque would place this clearly autobiographical passage on the evening of August 8 1925, when the peloton had just completed the gruelling 270-kilometre stage in the summer heat riding from Pamplona, and were preparing for the third and final stage the following day – the 173-kilometre run to Bilbao.

We know for a fact that for much of August 1925 Hemingway was working away on *The Sun Also Rises*, on his own, in the genteel peace and quiet of San Sebastian.

The leader referred to – the poor unfortunate suffering from boils – was almost certainly Belgium's Auguste Verdyck, who clinched the overall victory the following day by winning the third and final stage.

Verdyck had finished eighth at the Tour de France earlier that year. The 1925 Tour of the Basque Country – only the second edition in the race's history – was dominated by Belgian riders, with Joseph Pe winning stage one from Bilbao to Pamplona and Félix Sellier taking stage two from Pamplona to San Sebastian.

The enduring mystery, or at least debating point, concerning Hemingway and road cycling is of course his lionising of Bartolomeo Aymo (also spelled 'Aimo') by blatantly using the Italian rider's name for the small but key character of the heroic Italian ambulance driver in *A Farewell to Arms* – arguably Hemingway's most critically acclaimed novel. It's worth remembering right at the outset that Hemingway himself had travelled to Europe from Oak Park, Illinois to volunteer as an ambulance driver for the Red Cross on the Italian front before he was badly injured by an exploding shell during one of his first visits to the combat zone. So the depiction of this particular character would have been close to his heart. He would have been at great pains to get it right.

His mythical fictional character of Aymo is a 'good sort'. During the retreat from Caporetto, he rummages tirelessly to find food and supplies for the others, and works prodigiously to try to free the ambulance from the clawing mud. Displaying a virtuous side that can go missing in the theatre of battle, where the spoils of war are ravenously consumed, Aymo chooses not to force himself on two attractive young women he encounters, and instead decides to feed them. And then, suddenly, in the confusion of retreat, he dies a violent and random accidental death at the hands of the Italian Army – collateral damage to use today's appallingly impersonal terminology. The reader's sympathies are almost totally with the gallant but unlucky Italian ambulance driver.

This selection of Aymo, who achieved a literary immortality way in excess of his sporting legacy, is therefore a big call on the author's part. Yes, Hemingway clearly needed to find a suitable generic Italian name, but to opt for a current professional cyclist who was still one year short of retirement when the book was published in 1929 seems a tad unusual to say the least.

Not that Hemingway had ever hesitated to pluck names from the sporting record books for his own use. In *The Sun Also Rises*, as the plot developed in the second half of the book, and he needed a handsome matador who the nymphomaniac Brett Ashley would feel absolutely compelled to seduce, he suddenly

changed the matador's 'working name' of Niño
de la Palma – in reality a talented but unattractive-
looking contemporary matador – to the much more
historically revered fighter Guerrita. But then, having
delved into the history books, he was much taken
with Pedro Romero from the late 18th and early 19th
century when he was reportedly the most handsome,
stylish, romantic and admired matador in the sport.
So the name Guerrita was promptly binned and
Pedro Romero it was.

For Hemingway, rightly hopeful that *A Farewell to
Arms* would be read widely in Italy and cycling-mad
France, to deliberately choose a well-known current
rider seems hugely relevant to me. The character in
the book would automatically take on the character-
istics of the athlete in real life, thus saving Hemingway the problem of having to spend valuable time
and space characterising the soldier in the book.

The choice of Aymo is in fact an effective and
logical extension of Hemingway's much-discussed
'iceberg theory' whereby if writer and reader are in
tune, you don't have to laboriously spell everything
out. In *Death in the Afternoon*, he explained his ice-
berg theory thus: 'If a writer of prose knows enough
about what he is writing about he may omit things
that he knows and the reader, if the writer is writing
truly enough, will have a feeling of those things as
strongly as though the writer had stated them. The
dignity of movement of an ice-berg is due to only

one-eighth of it being above water. A writer who omits things because he does not know them only makes hollow places in his writing.'

By brazenly name-checking Aymo, Hemingway was tapping into a considerable 'back story' that many will have been aware of, just as we were with Pedro Romero. If a picture can paint a thousand words, such a well-calculated name-check has got to be worth at least a chapter of unwritten words.

So, what kind of rider and man was Aymo? What was his 'story' and the assumed knowledge many of the book's readers would share? Well, he wasn't an absolutely stellar name, but he was nonetheless very much admired and recognised. Hemingway, it seems, deliberately steered clear of the Italian A-listers of the era – Costante Girardengo, Gaetano Belloni, Giovanni Brunero, Guiseppe Enrici, Ottavio Bottecchia, and of course Alfredo Binda – and opted instead for a perennial runner-up and nearly-man because that's exactly what he was looking for.

During the 1920s, Aymo finished on the podium at the Giro d'Italia four times (in 1921, '22, '23 and '28) without ever winning the race, and took two third places at the Tour de France (1925 and 1926). That is a considerable *palmarès* by any criteria, and to that we should add three stage wins at the Giro and two memorable mountain-stage victories at the Tour.

Within the sport itself, Aymo was a big name. He was a strong climber and very much a creature of

the Alps, where he particularly thrived on the epic
long, cold, misty climbs. It is noticeable that, when
he rode the Tour de France, he rarely featured in the
Pyrenean mountain stages. Perhaps he just didn't like
the hot sun and the sharper gradients, or perhaps he
was just too busy riding in a team role.

Aymo was a tenacious and loyal individual, and
a proven finisher of grand tours during an era when
a much smaller percentage of the starting peloton
actually finished the race. When he finished third at
the Giro in 1921, for example, only 27 of the original
69 starters made it to the finish in Milan after three
weeks of racing, while the following year, when he
was runner-up, only 15 of the 75 participants completed the course. The 1926 Tour de France, when
he finished third, was the longest in history at 5,745
kilometres, and on that occasion just 41 of the
126 starters found their way home. Durability and
reliability were his middle names.

He did win the then prestigious Giro del
Piemonte in 1923 – and claimed another three
podium places in subsequent editions – but, riding
in an ultra-competitive era, he invariably came up
just short in terms of overall wins. In short, he was
an early Raymond Poulidor – the French rider nicknamed 'The Eternal Second' – and in that respect
Hemingway showed a fine sensitivity and knowledge
of the sport in his choice. You don't have to be a
winner and 'the best' to be a hero in cycling.

Certainly when claiming his first two Giro podium places, Aymo was very much the junior partner at the Legnano-Pirelli team, expected to rein in personal ambition to assist the race winner both years, Giovanni Brunero, who was in any case an exceptionally talented rider and obvious team leader. It could have been that selfless work on behalf of another that was a large part of Aymo's appeal to Hemingway, and again in the 1926 Tour de France Aymo also rode largely in support of the runner-up, Nicolas Frantz – his team leader having moved to the high-profile Alycon team, who were hugely popular in France, winning the Tour with four separate riders in their trademark Kingfisher-blue jerseys.

At other times during his career, however, Aymo did have free rein to pursue his own dreams, but ultimately he was destined to fall just short of the ultimate reward, despite years of back-breaking toil. He was not really born to be a winner, but by never quitting he was still victorious.

A number of additional factors may also have kicked in for Hemingway. Surviving portrait pictures of Aymo depict a handsome and modest-looking individual with more than a whiff of movie-star charisma, and Hemingway was not above preferring aesthetically pleasing individuals in his books when it suited (again, as witnessed by his late switch to the dashing Pedro Romero in *The Sun Also Rises*). And weren't all ambulance drivers on the Italian front devilishly handsome fellows anyway?

On the subject of pictures, there are two famous moody images of Aymo's stage win from Nice to Briançon on the 1925 Tour that would surely have captured Hemingway's imagination as he avidly devoured the sports pages of the French press.

It was a brutal 275-kilometre Alpine day featuring the Col de Vars (2,108m), the Col d'Allos (2,250m) and the Col d'Izoard (2,360m), with the latter only having been raced twice before. The weather was downright rank, as many an Alpine summer's day can be, and the roads then were little more than mountain tracks.

Aymo was in his element, though, and the first image shows him riding out of the mist and ahead of the peloton at the top of the Allos. The second picture shows Aymo, although leading, dismounting and wearily walking his bike up the final rocky stages of the stark Izoard. Both images have a dissolute trench-warfare feel about them, and in the second, the smug race officials wrapped up in their warm clothes following Aymo in the comfort of their car add to its poignancy. Some people were born to suffer; others somehow escaped that fate.

Aymo enjoyed a huge personal success that day, taking line honours in 13 hours, five minutes and three seconds – nearly ten minutes ahead of runner-up Bottecchia.

Two days later, he was in good form as well,

finishing the 303-kilometre run from Briançon to Evian, which went over the Col du Galibier, with the same time as the stage winner. In 1926, he again dominated the Nice-to-Briançon stage, over the same route as the year before, this time beating Félix Sellier by more than six minutes, and the eventual Tour winner, Lucien Buysse, by 27 minutes.

And finally, the age issue. Born in Virle Piemonte in 1889, Aymo was 25 when World War One started, and is known to have raced as an amateur in Argentina in 1916, only turning professional in Europe when approaching the age of 30 in the summer of 1919, when organised racing recommenced after the war and he signed with the Ganna team.

When Hemingway was writing *A Farewell to Arms* in 1928, Aymo's final attempt to win a grand tour at the age of 39 at that year's Giro would have been big news and fresh in Hemingway's mind. Hemingway, as we have seen, habitually used 'working' names for his characters and only firmed them up in the final months before publication. If it was ever in doubt, Bartolomeo Aymo would have been confirmed as the ambulance driver at this stage.

Hemingway clearly identified strongly with Aymo. With over 200 pieces of shrapnel removed from his leg after his near-death experience in World War One, and with doctors digging out other fragments for years afterwards, Hemingway will have endured much discomfort and pain, especially as he remained

determined to pursue his sporting passions. By grit-
ting his teeth and 'never quitting', he could still be
'victorious', and by going his own way in the literary
world, and again 'never quitting', despite the many
rejections from publishers and editors early in his
writing career, he could be downright triumphant.

Hemingway also invested in Aymo an aesthetic
appreciation of the bike that very much mimics his
own. At one stage, the ambulance driver sees a group
of German helmets, which were 'bent forward and
moved smoothly, almost supernaturally along. As
they came off the bridge we saw them. They were
bicycle troops. I saw the faces of the first two. They
were ruddy and healthy-looking'.

And, of course, *A Farewell to Arms* contains the
famous quick-fire conversation between Aymo and
Bonello – a much more ruthless and less likeable
member of the ambulance driving corps.

'I wish to Christ we had bicycles,' says Bonello as
they labour to dig their ambulance out of the mud.

'A bicycle is a splendid thing,' agrees the ever-
optimistic Aymo.

At the end of *A Farewell to Arms*, the main character and narrator, Frederic Henry – the American
ambulance driver – muses on Aymo: 'I had liked him
as well as anyone I ever knew.' One way or another,
that sounds to me like a self-congratulatory slap on
the back by and for Hemingway.

In 'real life', Aymo seems to have virtually

disappeared after his retirement in 1930. Other than a brief obituary in *La Stampa* in 1970, which mentions that he subsequently ran a bike shop, nothing is known. Italian cycling journalists and historians have searched in vain, but to no avail. Nothing, for example, is known of his reaction to Hemingway hijacking his name. His disappearance from cycling circles seems as random and complete as his sudden death in *A Farewell to Arms*.

Elsewhere, Hemingway often flies the flag for cycling. His most-often quoted musing runs as follows: 'It is by riding a bicycle that you learn the contours of a country best, since you have to sweat up the hills and coast down them. Thus you remember them as they actually are, while in a motor car only a high hill impresses you, and you have no such accurate remembrance of country you have driven through as you gain by riding a bicycle.'

That comes from an article in *Colliers* in September 1944 when he also recalled cycling days around Paris: 'I knew the country and the roads around Epernon, Rambouillet, Trappes and Versailles well, as I had bicycled, walked and driven a car through this part of France for many years.'

In *Islands in the Stream*, artist Thomas Hudson, yet another Hemingway alter ego, recalls: 'A bicycle was more fun than a motorcar. You saw things better and it kept you in good shape.'

With his gammy leg and heavyweight boxer's

build, Hemingway was not ideally built for cycling. But the *Colliers* article offers up evidence of him cycling around Paris, and his friend – at the time anyway – John Dos Passos also recalls Hemingway the weekend warrior and 'Statto' in his memoir *The Best Times*: 'Hem was mad about cycling. He used to get himself up in a striped jumper like a contestant at the Tour de France and ride around the exterior boulevards with his knees up to his ears and his chin between the handlebars. Hem knew all the statistics and the names and the lives of the riders.'

In another tantalising hint that a big literary project on cycling from Hemingway might have been underway, Dos Passos also wrote: 'Now and then he would remember that I was a rival wordfellow and clam up or else warn me sharply that I mustn't do any writing about bicycle races. That was his domain.'

But having reluctantly concluded earlier that Hemingway's 'cycling classic' was probably never written, I now have a theory on Hemingway that might or might not stand academic scrutiny. It strikes me that in literary terms within the English speaking community, he virtually discovered marlin fishing and bullfighting. Certainly that was the case with the former, where he was among the pioneer 'sportsmen' to descend on the Gulf Stream and wrote with real authority and a palpable sense of discovery on the subject. Meanwhile, with the ancient sport of bullfighting, no English writer had gone into the minutiae in greater detail, and nobody had expounded with more eloquence on the psyche of the matador and the nobility of the bulls. Nobody had truly experienced – a favourite Hemingway expression – and then written about the chaotic life of a matador on the road during a scorching Spanish summer. What he wrote felt very new and cutting-edge.

Hemingway didn't like frauds, and was sensitive to being labelled as one himself. Objectively, there was no chance of that happening in either sport. You didn't have to agree with everything he said and some – notably Orson Welles on bullfighting – argued vociferously with him, but Hemingway had earned the right to write with authority. Very quickly he was a big fish in a small pond, which he found extremely pleasing.

With cycling, though, it was subtly different. It was a massive subject, and the Tour de France and Giro d'Italia were spawned by newspapers – the cherished love-children of journalists and professional wordsmiths. The races – and their heroes – were written about incessantly and obsessively by highly accomplished professional scribblers and camp followers who were at least as well acquainted with the vital inside track – 'the true gen', as Hemingway loved to call it – as ever he could be. As a voracious reader of the sports sections of French, Italian and Spanish newspapers – as well as specialist cycling publications such as *L'Auto* – Hemingway will have been well aware that his knowledge on the sport was not definitive.

Although knowledgeable and blessed with instinctive and possibly unmatched insight into the competitive male mind, when it came to cycling there was every chance of Hemingway being contradicted factually, along with his interpretation of tactics – which is not a prospect that would have greatly appealed given his prickly ego.

In short, the competition was extremely hot. Although his Spanish was more than serviceable and helped his understanding of the bullfighting scene, his French was reportedly always poor. In his Paris years, first Hadley and then Pauline used to take care of local chores, ordering meals, dealing with local tradesmen and paying bills. He struggled with the language – as he admits in *A Moveable Feast* – and was not the oracle, the go-to writer on the subject, although surely he could have become just such a guru figure had he stuck with it.

Or perhaps not. Perhaps for one of the few times in his life, he just bottled it. Cycling was too big a subject even for Hemingway.

Bibliography

The Sun Also Rises; *Men Without Women*; *A Farewell to Arms*; *A Moveable Feast*; *Islands in the Stream*; *Death in the Afternoon* – all by Ernest Hemingway.
The Best Times by John Dos Passos; *Papa Hemingway* by

AE Hotchner; *Hemingway: The Paris Years* by Michael Reynolds; *Hemingway: The Homecoming* by Michael Reynolds; *The Story of the Giro d'Italia* by Bill and Carol McGann
Website: Bikeraceinfo.com

Brendan Gallagher has been a sports journalist for 30 years, serving his apprenticeship in South Wales and as a director of Hayters Sports Agency before a 20-year stint at the coalface with the *Daily Telegraph*, proudly writing on any sport except football. He has ghosted Irish rugby union player Brian O'Driscoll's autobiography as well as *In Pursuit of Glory* and *On Tour* for Brad Wiggins and assisted with Nicole Cooke's *The Breakaway*. He also wrote the official LOCOG history of Great Britain and the Olympics and has penned a history of the Rugby World Cup. In a lighter vein, he indulged his love of comic-book heroes by compiling biographical histories of Wilson of the Wizard, Alf Tupper – the Tough of the Track – and Roy of the Rovers in *Sporting Supermen*. Currently working for *The Rugby Paper* and the Tour of Britain website.

5

Just like with Mark Cavendish, the British public's opinion of Bradley Wiggins seems to ebb and flow like the four seasons or the tide.

Here, **William Fotheringham** takes a closer look at Wiggo's farewell to top-level road cycling in 2015 at the cobbled Classic, Paris-Roubaix.

THE KNIGHT AND THE COBBLES

BY WILLIAM FOTHERINGHAM

Received journalistic wisdom is clear: the writer should steer clear of the reader responses at the foot of any article you have written that has been put up online.

But in the same way that I always had to pick my scabs when I was a kid, I can never help glancing at the views of the hardcore of *Guardian* readers who post whenever I write about Sir Bradley Wiggins.

Foremost among them are those who feel that the first British Tour de France winner and reigning world time trial champion receives way too much coverage in relation to his results, and that *The Guardian* has travelled a long way down the slippery path towards being little more than a Wiggo fanzine. So it was with the 2015 Paris-Roubaix, which the great man attempted to win – knowing all along it was a long shot – to mark his exit from Team Sky.

This is not the place to go into the broader debate on how *The Guardian* covers cycling, centring on whether the paper offers sufficient balance between the 'click-bait' stars – Wiggins, Cavendish, Froome,

Nibali – and those whose stories are clearly worth writing but might not up the page-views in the same way. But not every hardcore cycling fan out there viewed the way Wiggins staged his departure from Sky with the same rose-tinted views that coloured most of the coverage. And it leads into a health warning: if you felt there was too much Wiggo in the pages of *The Guardian* in April, turn to page 150 now.

The reasons why the man who would only finish 18th in the 2015 edition of Paris-Roubaix, having run ninth the previous year, could draw most of Fleet Street's finest to a Classic ran from the obvious to the more obscure.

To start with the obvious: since 2012, Wiggins has been catnip for the British media. To cite merely the UK contingent, Mark Cavendish, Ben Swift, Luke Rowe, Geraint Thomas and Ian Stannard are all better Classics riders in their various ways than Sir Brad, but they will never be seen greeting D-Day veterans, and won't be on *Desert Island Discs* any day soon. Like him or loathe him, the Marmite man of British cycling has attained national celebrity beyond anyone else.

However, if you removed the element of national celebrity from the equation, Wiggins's brief affair with Paris-Roubaix was also something that cycling cognoscenti could appreciate. The way a cycling champion opts to manage the final phase of his career can say much about him and his time.

Bernard Hinault's exit in 1986 was incisive, clinical. The pathetic way – in the best sense – in which Fausto Coppi and Eddy Merckx raged against the dying of the light summed up their inability to cope without the adrenaline surge of competition. The Armstrong comeback of 2009-10 was the perfect expression of his overwhelming hubris – so immense that it actually precipitated his final downfall – and the collective, shameless sense of entitlement of the stars of cycling's EPO years.

Wiggins's withdrawal from top-level cycling will be as gradual as that of Jacques Anquetil, but is unique for any Tour de France winner. The Brexit, or perhaps Wexit, began with Paris-Roubaix, after which he moved from Team Sky to his own UCI Continental squad, Team Wiggins. Afterwards came a series of races on home shores, varying from the Tour de Yorkshire in early May 2015 to a Cycling Time Trials 10-miler near Hull – amusingly a middlemarkers' race as Wiggins had not done an 'official' CTT race in the last ten years. That in turn led in to a successful attempt on the Hour Record and the final run-in to a hoped-for Olympic medal in Rio de Janeiro.

In having a date pre-set years out, Wiggins's departure is resonant of Hinault's long-expected party in November 1986, while the series of farewell appearances has hints of the last years of Anquetil's career in the 1960s. In any case, it should be light years distant from either Eddy Merckx's tearful acceptance of reality in spring 1978, or even Sean Kelly's transfer to the low-key, low-budget Catavana team in 1994.

As for what it said about the man himself, it underlined the importance of the Olympics and his constant need for new goals – not repeat ones – in an attempt to create the ultimate all-rounder's *palmarès*. Some of the things Wiggins does are forced on him by circumstance, but very little of his career has come down to pure chance.

The attempt to win Paris-Roubaix marked stage one of the Wexit, then, and a courageous one when put in context. Here was a Tour de France winner going completely counter to the typecast way in which his sport had progressed once the Merckx era ended in 1977-78. Wiggins was also going against the grain of the approach to cycling that had proved so fruitful for him over the years, trading the predictability of timed events – and stage races based on timed events – for the random nature of cycling's most capricious Classic. And he rode creditably on both his excursions onto the cobbles in 2014 and 2015, if not victoriously.

The argument over whether or not he might have won was fruitless because so many factors come into play at the end of a Classic, not least of which is experience (of which more later). But it meant he could leave Sky with his head high, on his own terms.

Only three Tour de France winners since Merckx have delved deeply into cycling's 'Hell': Hinault, LeMond and Laurent Fignon, all of whom were thrown into the race in their years riding for the great *directeur sportif* Cyrille Guimard. All three viewed Paris-Roubaix in radically different ways. In the Badger's case, this was the classic example of the personal challenge where there could only be one winner: him. *Je vais me l'avoir,'* he said: I'll have it. Hinault is remembered for his victory in 1981, wearing the rainbow stripes of world champion, but he was surprisingly consistent in Paris-Roubaix, finishing it five years in a row from 1978 to 1982, with a lowest placing of 13th.

Fignon shared the Merckx-Hinault view that a champion should be prepared to take on any challenge that presented itself – and remained utterly frustrated by his third place in 1988 – but for LeMond, the 'Hell of the North' was largely about the romance. It was one of three events that most motivated the American – the Tour and the world road championship being the others. This was hardly surprising, as they were the European races that received the most coverage in the US in the 1970s. Later, LeMond's romantic view of cycling's Hell was tinged with an awareness of the race's commercial potential: his use of RockShox mountain bike forks in the early 1990s leading to a brief period in which frame manufacturers explored the possibilities of suspension before largely reverting to convention.

By continuing to race to Roubaix into the 1990s, both LeMond and Fignon were aberrations as the sport became ever more specialised, its stars ever less willing to take risks, to the immense detriment of the two sectors at its core: the races and the riders. In the 1980s, riders such as Stephen Roche, Andy Hampsten and Joop Zoetemelk could be found on the Paris-Roubaix startline – and would make it to the velodrome – but, following the example of Miguel Indurain, in the following decade the Tour specialists turned their backs on Hell. Fignon rightly lambasted this development as part of the corpora-tisation of the sport, where the bean-counters saw tenth place in the Tour by a rider who had followed wheels for three weeks as being a greater return than risking that rider's season – and his chances in the Tour – on the cobbles.

* * *

More LeMond than Hinault in his sometimes ingen-uous approach to his sport, Wiggins called Paris-Roubaix 'the most special race for a road rider', and compared the cobbles – for their importance as part of the sport's heritage – to the Vigorelli velodrome in Milan, with the difference that the cobbles remain a going concern.

His attempt on Paris-Roubaix in 2015 was

infinitely more convincing than his bid in late spring 2014 to 'break America'. But it was a different answer to the same question – the great conundrum that bugged Lenin as the Winter Palace fell, and which you can imagine worrying Neil Armstrong as the lunar module bobbed around in the ocean on its return to earth: what do you do next when you have planned, schemed and driven for the biggest goals available, and nothing else will ever have the same allure?

The problem was already eating at the Tour winner in 2012 when we met at the British team base in Surrey a couple of days before he was to ring the bell in the Olympic stadium to open the London Games. The enormity of what he had achieved in France, and what it was about to bring in terms of national celebrity, were just dawning on him, because it was clear that, on paper, he was virtually certain to win the gold medal in the time trial.

Already, he was anticipating what he would say in June 2013: that a repeat Tour win was an objective too far given the demands he and Sky had made on his – and his family's – reserves of moral strength from 2010 to 2012. Among the alternative goals he floated was Paris-Roubaix, because of the example set by the man he had been pitting himself against in time trials since the prologue time trial of the Tour de France in London in 2007: Fabian Cancellara. The Swiss's time trialling ability had won him Paris-

Roubaix, and if Wiggins could surpass him against the watch, why could he not emulate him over the cobbles, in an event where on occasion sheer power can overcome tactical niceties?

In 2014, Wiggins returned to the Classic, but he did so in the same context in which he rode it for Garmin in 2009: in a state of almost existential uncertainty about what races he should be targeting as debate raged about whether he should ride the Tour de France for Sky.

'I was dropped on a mountain at Tirreno-Adriatico [in March 2014] because I was too heavy, so I went to Majorca and starved myself to lose weight to try to get selection for the Tour de France. Paris-Roubaix was just what I was doing; Ian [Stannard] broke his back, so I was put in the Tour of Flanders. I finished 30th [actually 32nd] after staying in the wheels all day and thought, "Bloody hell, I felt great there." So a week later I put myself in a better position [at Roubaix] and could have won it.'

This was not the rigid planning with which Sky has – unfairly – become synonymous. This was serendipity. There was a certain amount of scepticism that Wiggins had neither the bike-handling skills or the pure *cojones* to race over the cobbles, based on his nervous riding in the rain at the previous year's Giro d'Italia, but that ignored the reality: to survive the Tour's first week in 2012 you had to have balls, an instinct for the right moment to get out of trouble, and bike handling skill, while further back in 2010, the highlight of Sky's disastrous Tour was Wiggins, Steve Cummings and Geraint Thomas's textbook display of team riding on the cobbled stage into Arenberg.

After Paris-Roubaix in 2014, Wiggins felt that he or his companion from Sky in the final escape, Thomas, could have won the race.

'I froze in the finale. I was so focused up to the Carrefour de l'Arbre, and after I went across to the break with Tom Boonen and Niki Terpstra, I couldn't help it – the child in me came to the surface and I had to pinch myself a bit: was I really in the front group with ten kilometres to go, up there with the big names in a Classic? I was starstruck.'

'In 2014, [losing] was to do with [a lack of] experience,' said Servais Knaven, Sky's *directeur sportif* for the Classics. 'When Terpstra attacked, that was it, he was gone. You know if you go after him, you'll have another Quick Step rider on your wheel, so you need to react straight away, get away with two of you.'

'It was a huge step,' recalled Wiggins. 'The amount of times I'd stood in the velodrome having packed, watched the guys going for it and thought, "I'd love to do that." I should have talked more with Geraint. I remember being at the back of the group and staying there to the finish. I wasn't committed enough. It was all too much, really.'

A couple of months later, matters had moved on. Wiggins was not selected for the Tour due to Sky's need to focus their undivided attention on the 2013 winner Chris Froome. That in turn made it clear that his shelf life at the team was limited.

Although he had signed a handsome contract in the wake of his 2012 Tour win, there was no longer a place for Wiggins in their Tour squad as long as Froome remained in the team. The conundrum had mutated: the debate was still about which races he should target, but the issue now was how that would fit into an exit strategy from the team that had fought so hard to win his signature in 2009 and with which he had become synonymous.

A tilt at Paris-Roubaix ticked several boxes. Sky had often fallen short in the Classics and media attention around the team always focussed on the Tour de France; the presence of Wiggins at Flanders and Roubaix, with the interest he would bring with him, would recalibrate that a little at least.

The group of young British riders bred by Rod Ellingworth's British Cycling academy to excel at the Classics – Geraint Thomas, Ian Stannard, Luke Rowe, Andy Fenn – would benefit from a senior rider to divert some of the media pressure and bring in some extra horsepower. Wiggins needed to be kept away from Froome so a Classics programme was the answer there. And leaving Sky after the end of the greatest Classic of them all was a unique way to end his time at the top of the sport. You could even argue the plan had a touch of class to it.

* * *

For all his casual demeanour, Wiggins has always been a man who likes to get his teeth into a project. Talking to him three weeks out from Paris-Roubaix in 2015, he had clearly bought into the idea in the same way that he went lock, stock and barrel into Tim Kerrison's project for winning the Tour de France in 2012. During the winter, he rode over the final kilometres of the Roubaix route three times: in December 2014, January and February 2015, each time in a small group – with Bernhard Eisel, Christian Knees and Ian Stannard – due to Sky's other Classics men being absent at races such as the Tour Down Under and Tour of Qatar.

Together they rode the later sections of cobbles, from Denain to the finish, missing out the early stretches.

'We'd do the last 120 or 130 kilometres, which takes about five hours in December, so we would start just before Arenberg. We didn't look at the first five sectors, because to be honest nothing much happens there, although everyone goes absolutely eyeballs out for the first one – I've always wondered why they do that.

'The main one is Arenberg, coming out of there with no troubles. After that you've got the 100 guys who can do something; the 80 who had no chance have gone. After the second feed to the finish, the

50 guys who can do something are left; the ones who are just dreaming have gone.

'It's really beneficial doing it when the roads are empty. When you do the usual recon on the Wednesday before the race, there are so many people around, so much going on, that you can take your eye off what you are supposed to be looking at. When you put a load of spectators on a cobbled sector, that changes it.'

'It was probably more recons than you would usually do,' admitted Knaven. 'Brad and I spoke about it and said it would be good to do. You end up knowing the route, what's coming, where to move up before you come to the cobbles. It helps because often the car is too far back for the radios to work. You can also test the bike, tyre pressures and so on. We were lucky because it rained a bit the first time so we could ride in the mud – it meant they had that experience as well.'

'It was good to see it in bad conditions,' said Wiggins. 'The first sector we were just creeping over them [the cobbles] because we didn't know what to expect, but by the end of the day we were pressing on a lot more. It was like a mountain bike ride where you start cautiously and get really confident by the end, just flying over everything, feeling the back end of the bike jumping about.'

The team that had helped him build up to the Tour in 2012 was re-united, or most of it: Tim Kerrison for physiology, British Cycling expert Nigel Mitchell for nutrition, a British Cycling conditioning coach. By April 2015, Wiggins was weighing in at 77 kilograms – five heavier than he had been when he won the world time trial title the previous September and seven more than when he won the Tour in 2012.

'I'm back where I was when I rode the track. You can carry an extra one-and-a-half to two kilograms of fat, and I've put on four or five kilograms of upper body muscle so I'm not as fragile. You need the upper body strength to fight for position more, sprint up the climbs out of the saddle. I never had that before.

'Tim and I worked out the demands, but a lot came from me to start with,' explained Wiggins. 'It's not about power-to-weight ratio, and it's not like a time trial where you can predict pretty much where you are going to be. With these races I've trained specifically to their demands since the end of 2014. I based it on what I felt I needed from the races in 2014. I got all the video cassettes from my mum's, the ones I'd watched as a kid, and started timing all the sectors and the bits in between. The longest takes about five minutes.

'You get up to six hours, then you figure that the Carrefour de l'Arbre takes three minutes and 20 seconds, so it's simple: in a six-hour ride in the winter you try to produce the [high power] numbers at the end, because that's the business part of the race. It's simple to apply it to your training. It's simpler than the Tour de France, which is about saving energy for three weeks. This is all done in seven hours and then you get to go home.'

The other difference, Wiggins said, was that Paris-Roubaix – and other cobbled Classics – are simply less 'quantifiable' as targets compared to the world time trial championships and Tour de France.

'I've been saying all winter it's not a given. I was talking to Sep Vanmarcke and he said, "If you read the press, you've already won," but if it was as easy as that I'd have done it 15 years ago. It's not a lottery, because you have to put yourself in the best position. You can be in the best shape and finish last – Greg Van Avermaet crashed last year on a silly corner and was out.'

Preparing for Het Nieuwsblad, the Tour of Flanders and Paris-Roubaix in the winter of 2014-2015 was, Wiggins said, a different matter to building for the Tour; it was back to the old Kerrison principle of breaking down the demands of the event and training for them. One factor he had trained for, he explained, was 'the explosiveness of the race. The sectors are mainly between one minute and two minutes – in Flanders they are shorter – so what you try to do is put out explosive power for a minute followed by riding at threshold. It's the repetitive nature of that which is tough.

'It's easy going to Majorca and putting the numbers out up the climbs [to prepare for the Tour]. These races are predominantly flat so it's harder to train for: you have to produce the power on your road bike. And it's not a matter of battering around Majorca on your time trial set-up. This morning I did two times 20 minutes at threshold on a local time trial course, but on the road bike, trying to be comfortable on it in that old Hugh Porter pursuiting position, because if you find yourself off the front with three kilometres to go it becomes a time trial and you don't want to be out of your comfort zone. So 90 per cent of the work this winter has been on the road bike – I got on my time trial bike for the first time four days out from Paris-Nice and it showed.'

All this, he said, meant that as the day approached, he was clearly in better physical condition than he had been coming into the 2014 race, so he should, on paper, be capable of improving on that ride. But there was one final factor: his head.

'It's about committing on the day. You've all seen it: when I'm committed I'm right in there; when I'm not, I'm dawdling at the back being dropped on climbs. The good thing for me is that there is no excuse not to do it. In the past there were always reasons – looking to the Tour, Romandie, the Dauphiné – but doing the Hour Record seven weeks later is no reason to sit up in Roubaix.

'You have to put yourself in position for the sectors. When you approach Arenberg or – in the

Tour of Flanders – the Kwaremont, you're going at
65 kilometres per hour, counting down the distance
– 300 metres to get there, 200, 100. You know you
are going to hit them at 60kph, and if you are fifth
or tenth wheel you will be okay. If you're in 20th you
start thinking it's not fun any more and that's when
you slip back. That's where the commitment comes
in. You have to put everything out of your mind.
You have to be willing to die for the cause.'

* * *

As Knaven said, winning a Classic all depends on
the circumstances of the race, and the cards turned
one by one against Sky at Paris-Roubaix on April
12, 2015. Wiggins was ill in the week before the
final run-in, cancelling his scheduled start in the
Grand Prix E3 Harelbeke after much uncertainty.
Thirty-six hours before the race, he was sufficiently
grumpy and stressed that he attempted to cancel his
pre-race press conference, only to be dragged out of
his hotel room for ten minutes in which, paradox-
ically, he gave a bravura performance. Having won
the time trial at the Three Days of De Panne – his
last win in a Sky jersey – a crash at Flanders left him
'beaten up' and on the back foot, where in 2014 his
32nd place was a welcome surprise.

Before Roubaix, Wiggins had made much of
the fact that Sky could expect to have 'numbers' in

the finale, with Rowe and Thomas on coruscating form. But the body blow came when Thomas was squeezed up against a kerb in the village of Wallers with 93.5 kilometres to go, just after the Arenberg forest. He fell heavily and that was that: a team eviscerated. But 60 kilometres later came the one moment during the relatively short sector of cobbles at Moulin de Vertain, however, when the cycling world got to see something it has rarely witnessed: Wiggins unleashed and on the attack, after he went clear of the lead group to link up with Stijn Vandenbergh and Jens Debusschere, with Zdenek Stybar joining the trio. It was abortive, but briefly, as the lead opened to 15 seconds, it looked as if it might lead to something significant.

'Brad knew his best chance was to try something, and he did it at a moment when no one expected it,' said Knaven. 'But you could see that when he moved everyone was watching and chasing, even Wanty. It was the perfect moment, but Stybar was with him and everybody got nervous. He had a clean run – no crashes, no punctures and he was able to move up in the finale. I was surprised it was a big group together; it looked as if no one had the legs. Normally when you get to Wandignies [zone 16] with this wind, it splits in pieces. We didn't have a lot of luck, but there wasn't much co-operation when the [early] break had ten minutes. We took responsibility but teams like Giant and BMC said they didn't want to ride. It's a bit weird when Cancellara and Boonen aren't here.'

There was another brief flurry five kilometres out when Wiggins went clear with Vanmarcke in pursuit of eighth place – Degenkolb and the rest of the winning move being clear – and his attempt to lead in the group for tenth on the velodrome was also doomed. He took what consolation he could: a trouble-free race, being in among the action and eighth place for team-mate Luke Rowe.

Wiggins appeared at the door of his team bus afterwards to more of the cheers that had accompanied him since the start in Compiègne.

'I was pleased with the race. It was nice to be able to attack. I had a go where I said I would in the morning to the team. It was good; I was just lumbered with a couple of people who didn't want to work. I think the right winner won in [John] Degenkolb. It was a bit soft – a bit "looking at each other". It didn't go on force, not like a classic Roubaix. That was a shame – it would have nice to have a proper one à la Ballerini 20 years ago.'

'It could have been any one of us [who won]. They said afterwards on the bus that when I went it was like panic stations. I guess that's a bit of the hype, saying you're up for it. When I attacked I was right up the motorbikes – it was like being 16 again out training, thinking I was it. It was nice. It's something to tell the kids: your dad was shit at Paris-Roubaix, but at one stage he was ahead of the main group.'

At his first race post-Sky, post-Roubaix – the Tour de Yorkshire – Wiggins seemed more relaxed, almost relieved at the change of milieu and pace – the small camper van after the big black bus. Reading between the lines of what he was saying about the foundation of Team Wiggins, and talking to those close to him, you could understand his change of mood and demeanour. Historically, throughout his career, he has been a rider who aims for a major target, hits it, and moves on, usually with a gap while he recoups and decides on the next goal. It is a *modus operandi* that worked perfectly for a track racer with his sights on Olympic gold medals, but which had always fitted uneasily with the sustained pressure of road racing.

In his five-and-a-half years riding for Sky, Wiggins functioned at his best for just 20 months – from the end of 2010 to August 2012. It was a period bookended by the utter disillusionment of the 2010 Tour of Lombardy, after which he checked out of the team's hotel – fibbing that he had changed his flight – to go and drink on his own, and the bizarre 2012 Tour of Britain, where the tensions within Sky after the Tour de France came to a head, with the farcical sight of the Tour winner coming to a full stop on a Staffordshire moor to wait when his designated team leader, Mark Cavendish, had been dropped. There is, perhaps, food for thought here for Dave Brailsford. If Wiggins's talent was not used to its fullest in those years, could the same be said of other riders within Sky, and, if so, why?

The Sky model can seem relentless compared to the way other teams operate: the spells incarcerated on Mount Teide in Tenerife, the constant media focus, the need to stay 'on message' in the corporate machine. The intensity and work ethic within Sky brought Wiggins everything he dreamed of, but he and his team only truly worked in harmony for that brief spell. There were other factors in the un-coupling: the obvious conflict and unease he felt at becoming part of the UK celebrity machine after his stellar 2012 and the undercurrent of conflict over leadership with Froome and those around him, which rumbled on through 2013 and 2014.

'It's relentless,' he said of life at Sky in the spring of 2015. 'I've had three or four really intense years. I thought last year [in 2014] that it would be nice to have fun racing and enjoy riding my bike because there was a lot of time when it wasn't [enjoyable].' That mission at least was achieved in the run-in to Paris-Roubaix, he believed.

'We've had a good time. We were joking the oth-er day, "You poor sods have got to go and ride [in] the Tour team now; it's all miserable and depressed because you've got to lose weight," and they were all like, "Don't remind me of it." In years to come I'll look back on these times with affection. It's just a shame it's got to come to an end.'

It was, he said, 'a new job, a bit of a hobby, a bit of passion.'

In one sense, his failure to win was a reassuring reminder of why the great Classics remain so special. If a rider with the right engine could spend most of his career eschewing the attacks and counter-attacks and essential uncertainties of one-day racing, then just put together a good plan and turn up at Paris-Roubaix and win, that would devalue the Monuments. Wiggins felt no regrets that he had left this all so late; too late to gain the experience and tactical instincts that make the perfect one-day racer, so late that he could not come back again and use what he had learned for one more go. 'Naaah. Not now. I've had a good run. I had my opportunity 12 years ago.'

But in years to come, when he reviews his stellar career and looks at the only gap amongst the gold medals, stage-race triumphs and records, perhaps the Knight of the Realm will wonder whether he really should have left chasing the cobbled trophy until it seemed like almost an afterthought. Wiggins the Classics-hunter was epitomised by that late attack outside Moulin de Vertain: it was stirring to watch, but it was all too brief.

William Fotheringham is cycling correspondent at *The Guardian* and the author of best-selling biographies of Tom Simpson, Fausto Coppi and Eddy Merckx. His latest book, *Bernard Hinault and the Fall and Rise of French Cycling*, was published in May 2015.

6

With its 21 hairpin bends, each bearing the name of the riders that have triumphed on its slopes, Alpe d'Huez is arguably the Tour de France's most iconic climb.

Peter Cossins sits down with Hennie Kuiper – twice a Tour-stage winner on the Alpe – and discovers a man who knows those famous hairpins like the back of his hand.

DUTCH MOUNTAIN

BY PETER COSSINS

'I know that mountain like my pocket. But this story is too important to make an article over the phone. When you really want to write about what I can tell about the history of the Alpe, we have to see each other.'

When you're writing a book about Alpe d'Huez, an opportunity to meet the first man to win twice on what is undoubtedly cycling's most renowned climb is too good to miss, even if it does happen to arrive after you've submitted the final draft of the book. I had been trying to get hold of Hennie Kuiper for some time, but even though the Dutchman has ostensibly retired, his schedule is still busy. There are speaking engagements, PR commitments and media duties. He tells me he's got two spare hours on a Friday afternoon in early May, so I quickly book myself in to see arguably the best rider never to win the Tour de France.

For many fans, Kuiper is probably best remembered as a two-time winner on Alpe d'Huez and as the *directeur sportif* who was in the Motorola team car behind Andy Hampsten when he won on the Alpe in 1992, and then guided Lance Armstrong through the first years of his career at that same team. However, his lofty place in the sport's hierarchy comes thanks to his other achievements. Olympic road race champion at Munich in 1972, for which he prepared by winning the Milk Race, he went on to take the Dutch title and world crown in Belgium in 1975, won four of the five Monuments (and finished second in the other), and was twice runner-up in the Tour de France.

Kuiper was not only a man for all seasons, but a rider for every kind of terrain. I can't think of another Alpe d'Huez victor who would insist, 'Paris-Roubaix? Now that was my race.'

Kuiper lives in the tidy suburb of Lonneker on the edge of Enschede in northern Holland. Pictures of some of his greatest moments hang in his office, while his loft has been converted into what he describes as 'my little museum'. A clothes rail runs along one side. Hanging from it are dozens of team and classification jerseys. He runs his hand along it, looking for a particular jersey.

'Here we are – 1972. And here's the leader's jersey from the Milk Race.'

A couple of hangers along the rail is his Dutch team jersey from the Munich Games. On the other side of the room is the bike on which he won that Olympic gold. There are stories all around us, but I'd need much more than two hours to hear them, and that's time I need to hear Kuiper's memories of Alpe d'Huez.

* * *

When I began work on the book, rather than presenting a straightforward and ultimately quite dull record of who won when on the Alpe, and how they did it, I wanted to put together what is effectively a biography of the climb. It includes everything from its geology and ancient history, including the short spell in the Middle Ages when silver mining close to the current resort's heliport and beach volleyball court made it the highest permanently habited settlement in Europe, to the Dutch radio commentator whose hugely popular reports were not only over the top but also bore no relation to what was actually happening in the race. The aim was to create a picture of how Alpe d'Huez became so famous that it is now fair to say that, unlike anywhere else except Paris, the Tour de France needs it just as much as the resort needs the Tour.

Running as a thread through the book is a report of the 1976 Tour stage between Divonne Les Bains and Alpe d'Huez. Although it was the race's second visit to the mountain after Fausto Coppi's success way back in 1952, the Italian's romp didn't signal the start of what would eventually become the long-standing love affair between race and climb.

Indeed, the general consensus on the Tour's first-ever summit finish was that it was ill thought out and too selective. The bunch rode in a sheep-like flock for more than 200 kilometres, prevented from straying by pump-wielding shepherds such as Raphaël Geminiani and Lucien Lazaridès, who insisted on their peers preserving their resources until the unprecedented final test.

When the bunch reached the Alpe's initial ramps, which are the steepest on the mountain, a brief flurry of attacks ended with Coppi riding across to Jean Robic, then stretching the Frenchman to his limit, before easing away to victory and a yellow jersey he kept all the way to Paris.

'The organisers ought to be examined by a psychiatrist,' was one damning verdict on the race's lofty innovation.

Tour director Jacques Goddet may not have taken up this advice, but the Tour's immediate shift away from summit finishes confirmed that he hadn't been impressed with Alpe d'Huez, either.

He adjusted this stance only gradually, including the occasional summit – usually the Puy de Dôme – until television began to have more of an influence on his route planning from the early 1970s. By that point, the tendency for the bunch to sit tight until the final climb, which had previously been derided, became an advantage.

In the new TV era, both race and television

directors wanted the action condensed into short set pieces guaranteed to attract the greatest audience.

For Goddet and Tour co-director Félix Lévitan, the return to Alpe d'Huez in 1976 fitted perfectly with this, and was also intended as a reprise of the battle fought out in the Alps the previous summer between Eddy Merckx and Bernard Thévenet.

Although this plan went awry when Merckx came out of the Giro with an open wound several centimetres long on one of his buttocks, Belgium still offered the biggest threat to Thévenet's defence of the yellow jersey in the shape of three-time Grand Prix de la Montagne winner Lucien Van Impe and Tour debutant Freddy Maertens. The Dutch challenge was potent, too, headed by Joop Zoetemelk – the favourite for many in Merckx's absence, including the five-time champion himself – and world champion Kuiper at the head of the powerful TI-Raleigh team.

The race's first week ran to a familiar pattern. The sprinters dominated, or at least Maertens did. The bristlingly powerful Belgian won two stages, as well as the prologue and a 37-kilometre time trial, to open up a lead of four minutes on all of the yellow-jersey favourites going into the rest day at Divonne. As the Tour headed out of the spa town near Geneva on another sweltering morning in that summer of record temperatures, Van Impe sidled up alongside the race leader.

'I'm going to attack as soon as we reach the foot of Alpe d'Huez,' Van Impe warned his compatriot.

'I'm ready,' Maertens replied.

'Fast Freddy' had indeed done all that was possible to be ready. He'd spent two weeks at Alpe d'Huez with his best friend and team-mate Michel Pollentier the previous December. The pair had ridden the climb as often as the winter weather allowed, until Maertens felt he'd cracked it – that he could hold his own on the 13.8-kilometre ascent from Bourg d'Oisans. He was confident he could contend for a high overall finish in Paris.

This may seem unlikely in these days when specialist sprinters are precisely that, but Maertens was not alone in believing he could challenge the mountain goats. Five-time Tour winner Jacques Anquetil declared that, with a four-minute cushion as the race headed towards Alpe d'Huez, the Belgian could emulate Merckx and win the Tour on his debut, while L'Équipe's illustrious chief correspondent, Pierre Chany, also suggested Maertens could hold the lead through to the key stages in the Pyrenees.

Nowadays, even key domestiques are sure to be well acquainted with any key climb on the Tour menu, whether it has featured before or not. However, like Van Impe, Zoetemelk and Thévenet, Kuiper confesses that his knowledge of Alpe d'Huez was limited to what he read about it in the roadbook on the rest day. His compatriot Zoetemelk saw enough in that description to decide to swap to a lighter bike just before the ramp up to the first of the climb's 21 hairpins, which had already been numbered in descending order from the bottom at the instigation of local hotelier Georges Rajon – one of the prime movers behind the Alpe's hosting of the race in both 1952 and its return in the 1970s.

'Freddy was still the leader and in good shape when we came to Alpe d'Huez,' says Kuiper. 'I remember [Gianbattista] Baronchelli made an attack up towards what is now the Coppi turn [21]. Maybe I was feeling a little stressed or I was dreaming too much about the yellow jersey, but my legs were blocked. It was horrible all the way up the climb. There was no way I could stay with the leaders.'

Kuiper confesses that his humiliation that day was completed when Maertens passed him as he rode under the red flag with a kilometre to go.

'I was a much better climber than him. Just before the Tour, I'd won the Tour of Switzerland. I'd won the stage on the Gaflei in Liechtenstein, which has sections of 25 per cent, so when I saw Freddy ride past me, I was so mad with myself. I went straight on the attack on the next stage to Sestrières, which was stupid, but I had to get rid of my aggression. I rode on the front with four or five guys on my wheel without even thinking about what I was doing. It was crazy,' he admits.

Kuiper had another go at rescuing something

from the wreckage of his first concerted attempt on the Tour's overall classification when a few days later the race sped into St Gaudens, in the foothills of the Pyrenees, on the day of his parents' 40th wedding anniversary.

'There was a big party in Holland that day for them, so I tried to win the stage. There was a small group of us just ahead of the peloton coming into St Gaudens, and I came around the last bend too aggressively, my front wheel slipped away and I crashed so hard. Somewhere there's a picture of me sitting on the ground with blood pouring out of my head and the peloton passing by on both sides of me,' he says.

Kuiper spent the long train journey back home with fellow TI-Raleigh retiree Gerrie Knetemann mulling over his failure to perform. He maintains it came down to one overriding factor: experience or, more precisely, his lack of it – both in relation to the Tour and to Alpe d'Huez.

'I did two Tours of Italy and a Vuelta before I took on the Tour because my respect for the Tour was so big. Sometimes I can't believe how they put young riders straight into the Tour and even make them the leader of the team, like Wilco Kelderman, for example. The Tour is so hard, and not only on your legs. You have to be so strong in your mind as well, which is not easy when you're young,' he explains.

'Experience is also the key to Alpe d'Huez,' he continues. 'I realised that when I rode it that first time in 1976. The stretches around bends 21, 20 and 19 are the toughest, but most people forget that the sections up in the meadows around bends four, three, two and one are also difficult. You have to know the mountain in order to work out where it's best to ease off, where you can make up ground, where it's best to attack. Knowing whether it's best to go on the inside or the outside of turns is also very important.

'It's a particularly difficult climb for riders who like to keep to one tempo. I could cope with it fine because I could accelerate and spend a long time dancing on the pedals if I needed to. But for Tour contenders like Jan Ullrich or Stephen Roche, who liked to keep riding at one steady speed, Alpe d'Huez was a real problem.

'The first ramp is very steep, then you get to turn 21 and it's almost flat and your legs suddenly start spinning. Then you start climbing steeply again, and it's the same story at turn 20. A bit higher up the climb the gradient eases off, and that's also the case at Dutch corner [seven]. Those are the sections where you've got to be confident if you're aiming to make an attack. That's where I attacked in '77.'

The Dutchman explains how he fed off his setback at Alpe d'Huez in 1976 to prepare himself for 'a show of revenge' 12 months later.

'Every rider needs to find the best way of

organising his energy, his motivation. For me, it was that moment. I spent a year dreaming of Alpe d'Huez,' he recalls.

The 1977 race, which was three-and-a-half weeks long, lacked spark until well into the final week – until the Alpe d'Huez stage, in fact. Tour debutant Didi Thurau, who was Kuiper's TI-Raleigh teammate, was the main talking point, racking up four stage wins during his two weeks in the yellow jersey. But the media were scathing about the lack of action among the main contenders, who included Merckx in what would turn out to be his final Tour.

'I knew that the stage to Alpe d'Huez, which went over the Madeleine and Glandon, was the one for me. I was feeling in such good shape, which encouraged me to make an attack on the Glandon. Merckx was like, "Hey, are you crazy?" But Eddy lost eight or 12 minutes that day. He was already feeling his bad legs. We continued up, and Van Impe made an attack about four or five kilometres from the top. He wasn't so far ahead – maybe 30 or 40 seconds. Then up came Maurice de Muer, Thévenet's sports director, and he told him: "Stop – don't work if Zoetemelk's not working." And what happened then was that Van Impe got one minute, two minutes, three minutes. Eventually, Thévenet made his own decision. He said, "The sports director says it's fine, but I'm losing the Tour here." So he started to work.'

In an interview with the Frenchman, Thévenet

told me he still felt aggrieved by the way Zoetemelk and Kuiper sat on while he did all the work chasing behind Van Impe. Afterwards, still furious with the lack of co-operation he received from the two Dutchman, he branded them 'arseholes' and 'little riders', but his performance in responding to them resulted in what he regards as 'the best day of my career'.

Kuiper, though, sees it very differently.

'Thévenet asked me to work, and I said, "Not me – you're the one in yellow." And Joop wouldn't work either. It was up to Thévenet to chase Van Impe. There was no reason for me to help him. After all, I wanted to win the Tour too,' he affirms.

When Van Impe – the best climber of his and arguably any generation – reached the foot of Alpe d'Huez, he led by three minutes. Just 33 seconds down on race leader Thévenet going into the stage, Van Impe appeared to be closing in on a successful defence of his title.

'But Van Impe made a mistake,' says Kuiper. 'I think if he hadn't gone on the attack, he would have won the Tour for a second time.

'But he's only a little guy, and he went hard from too far out on the downhill in a big gear, and then had to continue in that gear on the flat to the bottom of Alpe d'Huez. There was a headwind as well. That's so important to be aware of. Even now when I go to a bike race, I always listen to the radio to find out about the weather and the wind direction. Two of the factors that are most important in cycling are the rolling resistance of the road surface and the wind. The wind is almost always a factor in that valley, and Van Impe paid for being out in it on his own.'

After a very long and very slow build-up, the Tour had ignited on the Glandon. What came next would produce one of the most thrilling stage finales in its history. All four riders at the front of the race had a good shot at winning the title, with the odds very much in Van Impe's favour.

'We started up Alpe d'Huez and almost right away Joop made an attack. I was waiting to see what happened. Thévenet started pulling and got back up to Joop, and he immediately went into the lead, so we just sat there waiting. Van Impe's lead was still three minutes, but, with his focus set on gaining as big a lead as possible, I think he'd forgotten to eat. Joop went again and Thévenet did the same thing. I think Joop went at least one more time, and they were really big attacks; he was strong. Then we got up towards the second church, at what is now Dutch Corner, and I made my attack,' Kuiper explains.

'Just before I got to Van Impe, he had either had a crash due to being hit by a car or simply because he ran out of gas. It's still not clear what happened,' says Kuiper of an incident that has been the subject of a documentary in Belgium – *De Val*, released in 2014 (and available on YouTube), looking back at the nearest Belgium has come to winning the yellow jersey since Van Impe's 1976 success.

'There are two stories. The first is that a race organisation car hit him from behind. The second is that he was so tired he fell off. He certainly looked awful. It was very hot that day,' Kuiper recalls. 'His sports director, Henry Anglade, also made a big mistake, because he wasn't with him as I went past him standing there in the road waiting for a wheel. I was just focused on doing my own thing because I wanted to get a big piece of revenge after what had happened the year before.'

Kuiper confesses he also erred significantly high on the climb that day, and that his blunder may have cost him the overall title.

'The mistake I made, and that my sports director Peter Post, who was behind me, also made was not thinking or saying, "Go, go – you can take yellow." At that moment, after being so mad with myself the year before, the most important thing was to gain that retribution by winning the stage, but with a kilometre to go I was effectively in yellow. But in the final 500 metres, when I knew I'd got that revenge, that the stage victory was mine, I eased off a little.

'I had been totally entranced. I couldn't feel any pain. I had everything under control. But with 500 metres to go, I started to feel the pain; it was like someone had put something over my head and was trying to suffocate me.

'So I was so happy to get to the finish. Then I

found out I had missed the yellow jersey by eight seconds…'

Thévenet had managed to ride away from the flagging Zoetemelk, and then passed the stricken Van Impe, who encouraged the Frenchman to persist with his all-out effort.

'About 700 metres from the finish, I saw a friend of mine who told me, "You're going to keep the yellow jersey by one second." After that I did one hell of a sprint,' Thévenet had told me when describing how he pushed himself further than at any other point in his career – further even than when he famously beat Eddy Merckx at Pra Loup to win the Tour in 1975. 'I've always said that once I got to the line, I had absolutely nothing left to give. I couldn't have taken another pedal stroke. It was the day that I managed absolutely every little bit of energy I had in order to go as far as I physically could.'

Defending an advantage of 49 seconds over Kuiper, Thévenet yielded 41. He believes the often-quoted maxim that 'the Tour is won on the Alpe' was born that day.

'It's usually been the case that whoever has the yellow jersey at Alpe d'Huez wins the Tour de France. That means that everyone really fights to get the yellow jersey there, to have this slightly super-stitious belief working for them. If the stage were going to another ski station, they wouldn't have that thought in their heads at all. Alpe d'Huez instils the mentality, the desire, to fight with all that they have.'

Although the accuracy of this maxim is debatable, Kuiper agrees with Thévenet that keeping the yellow jersey that day made all the difference when it came to him winning the Tour for a second time.

'I think if I'd even finished one second ahead of Thévenet on GC [general classification] that day, I would have beaten him in the time trial and won the Tour. I rode a good time trial having prepared for it really well, but riding the final time trial of the Tour in the yellow jersey always gives a rider extra motivation – something extra in their legs,' he says.

Kuiper won on Alpe d'Huez in very different circumstances the following year, inheriting the victory after stage winner and new yellow jersey Michel Pollentier had been tossed out of the race for attempting to cheat the dope control. Speaking at the time, Kuiper confessed it didn't feel like a proper victory coming the way that it did, and it's clear he's not as proud of it as his 1977 triumph – apart from one aspect.

'Bernard Hinault was riding his first Tour, and he was on the front leading the chase behind Pollentier, with me on his wheel and then Joop. Hinault just kept pressing and Joop couldn't follow. Then I did something that I only managed to do once, and that was to drop Bernard Hinault. I made an attack, let him come back, and then I went again. That gave me a lot of confidence going into the rest day, with a big mountain day to follow. I made the king of the mountains jersey my target, and on that big stage I led over the Cucheron and then the Granier. But I pushed too hard on that descent, crashed and broke my collarbone,' says the Dutchman.

* * *

Kuiper and Zoetemelk may have failed to take the main prize in the 1970s, but their exploits on Alpe d'Huez, which continued when the latter claimed one of the two stages to finish on the mountain in 1979, encouraged ever-increasing numbers of their compatriots to head for the Alpe.

'The phenomenon of Dutch Corner started with those first visits to the Alpe in the mid to late '70s. Our victories caught the imagination of the Dutch people and media, and even of the French media. They would always ask: "How is it possible for you to be a climber when you come from a flat country?"

'The other thing was that cycling became more popular in Holland, and there was also more TV coverage. Everything came together. Joop won, I won twice, then Peter Winnen won twice, then Rooks and Theunisse – we had almost eight wins in a row. But now they talk about Dutch Mountain and it's 26 years since a Dutch rider won there. I think people are still proud of that, just as they are of Ajax winning the European Cup three times in succession in the 1970s, but the legend is rooted in the past.'

· And what of the role played by Theo Koomen in popularising Alpe d'Huez? Koomen's name may be unknown to most fans outside the Netherlands, but the Dutch national radio commentator's broadcasts have legendary status in his homeland, and his name often appeared in paint on the road up to Alpe d'Huez alongside the Dutch racing heroes. Combining the enthusiasm and machine-gun delivery of the Colombian commentators who broadcast from the Tour in the mid-1980s, Koomen also added a good dollop of complete make-believe.

Kuiper laughs.

'Of course I remember him. Nowadays it would be impossible to have a man like Theo Koomen, with all of the live coverage of the race. He made up some nice stories. He'd be having a coffee in France and saying, "Now we're behind the breakaway, and the fish are all jumping out of the pan…" He'd give the impression that the riders were attacking each other all day when we were still riding *piano*. He made it really interesting for his listeners. There's a recording of him commentating on a race I won and his commentary is non-stop: rat-tat-tat-tat-tat… He put all of his feeling into it, his personality. And doing that made everyone excited, which was good. I don't know whether he did it for his listeners or for himself, but he certainly transmitted what he felt watching the race. It must also have cost the Dutch economy a lot during lunchtimes because everyone would turn on to hear what he was saying. Everybody had a small transistor radio that was tuned to the Tour de France.'

Koomen's former colleague, Mart Smeets, who went on to become the face of Dutch TV's Tour coverage as presenter of the post-stage programme *De Avondetappe*, had told me, 'Koomen made everything up; he was good at that. If it was a dull stage, he would turn it into a tremendous stage... I'd be wondering if I was watching the same race as him.'

'How did you react?' I asked Smeets.

'I simply ignored what he was saying.'

Dismissive of Koomen's antics, Smeets was equally so of Alpe d'Huez's ongoing status as Dutch Mountain.

'How long is it since a Dutch rider did well over there?' he asked me, instantly providing the answer himself: 'Twenty-six years! So let's not talk about Dutch Mountain. It's a Dutch mountain in terms of colours on certain bends, and there are certain people of Dutch ancestry who act like drunken fools, but should you be proud of that? No!'

A veteran of 42 Tours, Smeets affirmed even as he admitted it hardly needed saying: 'I'm just not very fond of Alpe d'Huez. A Tour de France without Alpe d'Huez is heaven for this journalist.'

Kuiper acknowledges he has some sympathy for Smeets's anti-Alpe stance, although he still feels more attachment to the climb than any other.

'I don't like to see all this drinking and the mess it causes. You see the same thing at Paris-Roubaix,' he says. 'I hate those fans who only go to drink. It's like a holiday of drinking for them. They can end up causing accidents and someone could end up losing the Tour de France because of something stupid happening in these situations. Everyone seems to want to be involved in the race these days, but you have to respect the athletes, respect the effort they are making, let them get on with what they are being paid for, and let them take centre stage and take the glory. It is becoming a bit of a problem.'

Andy Hampsten, who won at Alpe d'Huez in 1992 and thrashed out at some fans on his way to the summit that day, described the experience as like 'trying to get through this vertical forest of people'. In the course of offering his explanation of what it takes to win and lose on the Alpe, the American had described how the fans who get closest to the riders tend to be the most drunk.

'They've got so much alcohol in their bodies that you can smell the odour of them sweating it out… They're out of their minds – so drunk that it turns into a bit of a guessing game. There is definitely an element of danger.'

Hampsten's analysis of the climb, in terms of its history, beauty and the challenge it offers, was particularly insightful. He insisted, though, that a

significant part of the credit for this should go to
Kuiper, who was in the team car behind him that
day and remains the only man to taste success on the
Alpe as a rider and as a *directeur sportif*.

Kuiper reveals that he didn't think he was cut out
for the job when he retired in 1988 at the age of 39.
But he got an offer to manage Team Stuttgart and
spent three years with the German outfit that later
morphed into Team Telekom. In 1992, he stepped
back up to the top level of the sport with Motorola.

'The first thing I should say is that Andy is a great
guy. I like to work with people, but my weakness is
that I'm too easy on them and sometimes you have
to be hard. But Andy was the type of person who,
when you gave him something, he accepted it with
both hands, whereas in the same situation a lot of
people only take advantage if you are easygoing.
While [TI-Raleigh team manager] Peter Post was like
steel, I was the direct opposite of that. But being like
that worked with Andy,' he admits.

'But I was really surprised when I went to
Motorola at how stressed he was. He didn't have a
great deal of confidence. It's always interesting to see
how athletes react when they're under pressure. Some
of them can't cope when they're told, "You've got
a good chance of winning today." Andy had a tendency to wait and think that he wasn't good enough,
so he always ended up getting beaten by guys like
Tony Rominger or Miguel Indurain. I was really keen

to see him win a mountain stage because he was certainly one of the best climbers, and on some days the very best. I told him that on the morning of the Alpe d'Huez stage.'

Tour legend has it that Kuiper went into Hampsten's room that morning and told him, 'Today is your day.' Neither man can remember exactly what was said, but both agree that they had been thinking about victory on Alpe d'Huez for some time. Hampsten said of Kuiper's role in his success that, rather than plotting out some great tactical master plan, the Dutchman kept things simple and focused on encouraging the Motorola team leader to follow up on his instincts. Both say the first key to that day's success was their agreement that Hampsten should follow any attack made on the Col de la Croix de Fer – the 2,067-metre pass that preceded the final ascent to Alpe d'Huez.

'We had Phil Anderson on the team, and Phil was a very good road captain. He was such a great professional. I loved him. When you told him to do something, he committed himself to it fully. He was so hard on himself from a physical point of view,' says Kuiper. 'He came back to get the last water-bottles to take up to Andy and I said to him, "Tell Andy that he ought to follow every attack on the Croix de Fer." It was always in his head that Indurain and those guys wouldn't let him go away, but not even Eddy Merckx went after every attack.

You just have to believe in yourself. A few minutes later I heard on the radio, "Attack by five riders," and Andy was one of them.'

Hampsten described the five-man move as 'a very good breakaway'. Along with him were French-man Éric Boyer, Belgium's Jan Nevens, Spaniard Jesús Montoya and Italy's Franco Vona. Hampsten regarded the latter as the major threat as Vona had been with Hampsten in the four-man group that had chased Claudio Chiappucci on his jaw-dropping ride up to Sestrières the day before.

Even at that point, Hampsten told me, he had made a point of assessing potential rivals for the run to Alpe d'Huez.

'It's often the case that the riders who win mountain stages are good riders but are just out of the picture a little bit in terms of the general classification. So, after I had finished exhausted at Sestrières, I stopped just after the finish line to catch my breath and to wait to see what the riders in the next groups were like because I knew that the Alpe d'Huez winner would probably be a very good climber who had perhaps taken it easy in a following group. But every one of the next ten or 15 riders I saw come across the line was absolutely knackered.

'They were shattered even though they might not have been chasing as hard as we had been, because it had been such a tough stage, so that made me feel better about how tired I was. I just thought, "Look,

I need a great night's sleep and to feel relaxed about the next day.'"

The problem for Hampsten was that even after making it into what became the winning break, he was anything but relaxed.

'They reached the foot of Alpe d'Huez with a lead of three minutes, but as we got onto the climb I could see that Andy was getting a little anxious,' Kuiper explains. 'I asked the commissaire if I could go up to him, and the mechanic in the car, who was an American like most of the other staff, said to me, "What are you doing? You can't talk to Andy now — he's too stressed." I was like, "Come on now. I want to give him good advice, I want to help him win the stage. You're crazy. Shut up, man!"

'I went up and told him, "Try to make an attack." Andy snapped back, "I can't do that!" I just said then, "Well, if you can't do that then you must try to push the speed up a little and you'll see what happens." What I said seemed to fit in with what he wanted to do as a little further up the mountain he pushed the pace up a little and suddenly there were four riders. It was beautiful to see. Then there were three, then just two — Andy was leading Vona — and then, without even getting out of the saddle, he pushed a little harder going through one of the bends and ended up by himself and flying towards the top. It was fantastic to see. It was good for me, too, to win a stage like that as a sports director.'

* * *

As time starts to run short, Kuiper takes me to see his 'small collection' in his attic, picking out pieces and pictures that have particular relevance to Alpe d'Huez. Talk of the greatest climb leads inevitably onto Kuiper's assessment of the greatest climbers.

'The real climbers were Van Impe, Lucho Herrera and Marco Pantani. When you saw them go away around a bend, you didn't know when you were going to see them again. Fuente was good, but he did stupid things,' he says, going on to recall an incident in the 1974 Giro when Eddy Merckx stripped off his rain jacket on a cold and dismal day purely with the aim of encouraging the brilliant but impulsive Spaniard José Manuel Fuente to attack.

'Off Fuente went, and he got a lead of several minutes. Then Eddy got his whole team – Jos Huysmans, Jos Bruyere, all those guys – chasing him down. I was a young rider watching all this, learning from it. On the last climb, we came around a corner and Fuente was weaving in the road in front of us. That was Merckx's plan all along, and it worked perfectly.'

Just before my time is up, and Kuiper has to head off to a meeting, I ask how he rated himself as rider.

'I wasn't a specialist in any area, but I was strong in the mountains, on the flat, in time trials – on every kind of terrain. I won some beautiful races, and I'm happy with, and proud of, my career. But I never quite managed to win the Tour,' he says.

I'll add that he's the only man to win on Alpe d'Huez and then guide another rider to success on that fabled ascent as a *directeur sportif*.

The contributing editor to *Procycling* and a contributor to *Cyclingnews.com*, Yorkshire-based writer **Peter Cossins** is the author of *Alpe d'Huez: Cycling's Greatest Climb* (Aurum Press, 2015) and *The Monuments: The Grit and the Glory of Cycling's Greatest One-Day Classics* (Bloomsbury, 2014, updated in paperback for 2015). He is also the co-author of *Two Days in Yorkshire* (Pavé, 2014), looking back at the 2014 Tour's Grand Départ, and is the translator of Christophe Bassons' *A Clean Break* (Bloomsbury, 2014).

7

The discovery of a 1957 Tour de France race programme prompts the question: just whose signatures are those that adorn its front cover?

The answer leads **Felix Lowe** on a journey back in time, to an age when men didn't wear helmets, and women played accordions on car roofs.

CAPTAIN ALEX

BY FELIX LOWE

Were it not for eBay, my knowledge of the 1957 Tour may not have stretched much beyond it being the first of five wins for Jacques Anquetil. Skimming through the annals reveals a veritable bonanza for the host nation: 20 stage wins (out of 24), a Frenchman in yellow from start to finish, the overall, points and team classifications, and – the only blot – second place in the mountains classification. Sweeping Gallic success unfathomable for us fans today.

Look closer and you'll see a large footnote. Stage 16 from Barcelona to Ax-les-Thermes on Sunday, July 14 – an otherwise routine day for the French with a one-two on Bastille Day – was overshadowed by the death of the French radio reporter Alex Virot, whose motorcycle careered into a ravine not far from the Catalonian town of Ripoll. For the first time in the Tour's 44-year history, a journalist had been killed in action.

At some point in the preceding fortnight – most likely at the *Grand Départ* in Nantes – Virot, and two

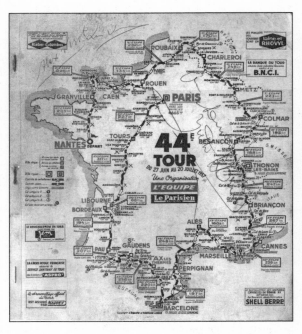

others, signed the cover of someone's official media guide. Bought on eBay for the mere price of a cinema ticket over half a century later, this very same programme fell into my lap in autumn 2014, opening the door to a story as gripping as any blockbuster at the local multiplex. Let me now share with you the world premiere of this tale of a true renaissance man – featuring, potentially, cameos by two mystery cast members from cycling's greatest show on earth.

* * *

It all started when a middle-aged sports memorabilia collector called Colin got in touch with a proposal.

'One of the most interesting items I have recently bought is a 1957 TDF programme superbly detailing the whole event,' he wrote. 'Bizarrely (or morbidly, depending on your viewpoint), it has been signed by a few people, including Alex Virot, the French journalist who was killed while covering the race. I'm trying to find out more about this accident. Perhaps you can help identify the other names and shed some light on the whole thing.'

Before meeting Colin, I needed to do some homework. I hadn't heard of this Virot chap, nor did my knowledge of the Tour stretch much beyond: 'Just who is that rider coming up behind? Because that looks like Roche! That looks like Stephen Roche!'

It soon struck me that to call Virot a mere pioneer of French radio broadcasting was doing him a gross disservice. The humble wireless seemed a mere front for his other alluring activities – such as winning an Olympic silver medal. (Between 1912 and 1948, special art competitions were part of the modern Olympic movement, offering medals across five categories: architecture, literature, music, painting and sculpture. Virot's *medaille d'argent* was for a football sketch from the 1928 Games in Amsterdam.)

Born in 1890, Virot lived his 67 years to the full.

After training with the prolific sculptor Antoine
Bourdelle in Paris, he made his name as an artist at
the magazine *Miroir des Sports* before becoming chief
caricaturist at the newspaper *L'Intransigeant* following
his Olympic success. Soon he was writing articles for
the paper and then, in 1929, he got his first break in
radio alongside his pal Jean Antoine.

Recovering from an inauspicious start (late to set
up, they had only just commenced their broadcast
when the peloton set off for the opening stage), the
pair would become – at least verbally – the Gary
Imlach and Ned Boulting of their time, with the
older Antoine anchoring proceedings while Virot
added vivid details about the riders and scenery.

Virot's 22 career Tours were littered with land-
marks: the Tour's first remote radio broadcast made
outside a studio (that damp squib with Antoine in
1929), the first live recording from a mountain stage
(1932, atop the Aubisque) and, in the same year, the
first package made from a plane (he was also a trained
pilot who fought during the First World War).

After landing a plush gig announcing the inaugu-
ral draw of the new national lottery in 1934, Virot
brushed shoulders with novelists Blaise Cendrars
and Colette while covering the maiden trans-Atlantic
voyage of the SS Normandie – the largest, fastest
passenger ship of its time. During a subsequent stay
in New York, he honed his journalistic techniques
at NBC. While irked by the rigidity of American

broadcasters, he became a keen advocate of wireless telegraphy (a precursor to the modern-day radio) and was instrumental in finessing its use back in Europe.

Besides cycling, Virot covered football, boxing, motor sports and skiing. As a war reporter, he covered the Italian invasion of Ethiopia and the Spanish Civil War. And, as you'd expect from such a man for all seasons, Virot was a key player in the Resistance for the Savoie Maquis in the Alps.

After the war, he returned to the radio waves: following brief stints at sports newspaper *L'Équipe* and French national broadcaster RTF, Virot joined Radio Luxembourg, where he worked until (and including) the day he died. As far as CVs go, Virot's seems complete to the extent of fictional.

Colin licked his chops as I reeled off the career highlights of this general master of all trades, jack of none. When filming a short snippet at the Rapha Cafe in London, I mused that Virot was Des Lynam, Phil Liggett, Dale Winton, John Simpson, Jimmy Doolittle and Rolf Harris all thrown into one (although Colin subsequently had the nous to edit out that last comparison).

Just days earlier, the mystery of one of the remaining two signatures had been solved: deciphering the first name of the scrawl, Colin had simply Googled 'Yvette + Tour de France' and – bingo! – some 575,000 results bearing the name Yvette Horner appeared. Among those, a review of John

Wilcockson's book *23 Days in July* (an inside account
of Lance Armstrong's seventh Tour sham in 2005)
by *New York Times* reporter Samuel Abt, who
reproached Wilcockson for mentioning the contro-
versial trainer Michele Ferrari 'on only two pages, the
same space given to Yvette Horner, defunct queen
of the accordion. Yvette Horner! She accompanied
the Tour decades ago, serenading the crowds who
gathered each night after a stage to watch in a town
square as a bed sheet was set up so movie films of
the race could be shown while moths danced in the
projector's beam. Those were the days...'

Quite how Horner – a five-foot-nothing accordionist from the sleepy town of Tarbes in south-west
France – became imbued in Tour folklore is a typical-
ly endearing quirk of the sport. The pint-sized Pyrenean was an integral part of the Tour *caravane* for 11
summers, from 1952, smiling beside stage winners
with a bouquet or sporting a sombrero on the roof
of a Citroën Traction Avant, dwarfed by her trusty
melodeon.

If Virot had his Olympic silver medal, then
Horner could go one better with boasts of world
champion status: in 1948 she became, aged 26, the
first women in history to win the feted accordion
World Cup. Sniffing out a PR opportunity, gas and
household appliances giant Calor approached this
talented, pretty, up-and-coming star to be the face of
their brand. Horner soon became a household name.

In a career spanning eight decades, she would sell over 30 million records and perform at an estimated 3,000 concerts. Such was her instant success at Calor that the accordion's answer to Edith Piaf was inevitably lured from the world of butane to the more glamorous realms of botanical bitters by the herbal *apéritif* brand Suze, upon whose car she became a mainstay for the next decade.

A manufactured cultural product who even had a footballer husband, Horner was the closest thing France would get to a modern-day reality TV star. The Tour became her tour – an annual pilgrimage to perform on a mobile stage accessible throughout France. She had the x-factor – striking a chord with a nation steeped in traditional, nostalgic values – and it was in representing brands that Horner herself became a brand.

Between these two icons, I had a slew of material for when Colin pressed the record button. The hook for our (very) amateur documentary was the eerie presence of Virot's signature on the 1957 programme just weeks – perhaps days – before his death. A dedication from a key figure of the *caravane* added another dimension, but the identity of the third name still remained unknown. To my untrained eyes, the blue-ink dash spelled out 'Jim' or 'Jean' ahead of a surname starting with the letter V. No handwriting specialist could help; two Tour historians were equally flummoxed. For hours I stared and squinted, hoping something would jump out. I waded through everything I could about the 1957 Tour, upturning nothing. Even my most most encyclopaedic follow-ers on Twitter hadn't a clue.

But it was okay. We had the stand-alone story of Virot – and the door was about to be flung open.

Alex Virot

Among the sparse viewers of our video was a Paris-based glass sculptor called Sophie Olchanski, who claimed to be Virot's grand-daughter. I had already made optimistic efforts to track down rela-tives by randomly contacting anyone with the name Virot on Twitter (no one had replied), so this was accordion music to my ears – a breakthrough in what was becoming an intriguing little side project.

Sophie promised me a selection of interesting

documents and photos relating to her grandfather's life. In return, she wanted help tracking down some archive footage. She answered a number of preliminary questions I sent over, but it wasn't easy, she said, because her father, Daniel Olchanski, had been dead for more than a decade. This threw me. Why would Virot's son have the surname Olchanski? It was my first question when we spoke on Skype.

'It's quite a strange story,' Sophie smiled. 'I can tell you now that no one actually knew Alexandre Virot had a son – even he didn't know at first. My father was illegitimate. Alex Virot was awfully handsome. He was having an affair with my grandmother but she was a married woman. My father was raised as the son of her husband, Roger-Angel Olchanski. So the name Virot did not continue.'

Olchanski was a industrialist in Paris who married Léontine Alice Bollack in February 1909.

'It wasn't like today,' Sophie said, sparking up a cigarette. 'People weren't married for *l'amour*. They were married in an intelligent way. It was convenient for them both. They respected each other a lot but they had their own lives.'

Alice (she preferred her second name) was just 17 when she married Olchanski, three years her senior. A beautiful young woman in high society, Alice hosted a traditional Parisian salon where she received writers, artists and poets. It was probably at one of these meetings that she met Virot – during his stint with Bourdelle. When she fell pregnant, she confided in Olchanski.

'There was no divorce and Olchanski agreed to raise Daniel – my father – as his own.'

It took a series of unforeseen circumstances for the truth to unravel. An influential political figure in France, Olchanski was also Jewish. When Jean, his oldest son, was taken in the Vel' d'Hiv round-up during the Occupation, the Germans wanted to trade father for son. De Gaulle and Churchill – both close to Olchanski – forbade any switch, encouraging him to travel south with his family on false identities.

'Because the Germans were looking for a couple and a child, they had to split up. Knowing that Alex was in the Resistance in the Alps, they sent my father – who was 13 at the time – to Savoie to be protected by him. He had to be hidden in a cow's carcass inside a butcher's truck for 24 hours.'

The plan worked. But while Daniel was safe in the Alps until the Liberation, Jean was sent to Auschwitz. He survived but felt betrayed, and never forgave his father for not rescuing him. After the war, he changed his surname to Olivier and moved to the south of France with his wife. How ironic that the brother who was a true Olchanski ended up dropping the name, whereas the other, by blood a Virot, would remain an Olchanski for life.

It took an unforeseen phone call from a man claiming to be 'Uncle Jean' for Sophie, then aged

17, to learn the truth about her grandfather. Daniel himself only made the discovery when he heard the locals gossip during his time in the mountains.

'All the village people recognised the likeness between them, and there was a lot of whispering that Alex was Daniel's father.'

There's no denying their resemblance. Among Sophie's photos there's a beautiful one of father and son sitting beside each other in an Alpine meadow. Daniel smiles and looks very much at ease, while Virot, in walking boots and socks to the knees, is topless, revealing a toned torso that belies his thick mane of white hair and the walking stick close to hand (he was now in his mid 50s).

'It was the start of a good relationship,' Sophie said. 'They stayed in touch after the war. Alex was a very good father for my dad.'

Daniel was 28 when he heard Virot's death announced on a news bulletin on television.

'It was a huge shock. He went to the funeral but he had to keep to the side because no one knew that Alex had a son. You know, it's hard for me,' Sophie sighed. 'They were so similar. There's a picture of the accident scene and it's horrible because all I can see is my father.'

That Sophie is haunted by this picture is hardly surprising. Taken from the road from which the motorbike plunged, it captures the aftermath of the crash on the dried-up riverbed 20 metres below.

It's a disconcertingly gruesome scene. Around 20 figures, including two clergymen, form a number of clusters. Some survey the tangled wreck; some stand above the twisted, lifeless bodies of Virot and his driver, René Wagner; others keep their distance, talk among themselves or face the other way, hands on hips, around shoulders or caught mid-gesticulation.

A shoe lies near the front wheel a few metres from Wagner, whose limp body looks rather neglected for someone who, according to reports, only died en route to hospital. A fractured skull killed Virot instantly. His face – easily recognisable because of his white hair – is tilted backwards, mouth agape and nose bloodied. A second stray shoe lies discarded beside his crumpled figure.

Around his shoulder, a familiar leather strap is attached to a pouch at his side – the case for his ubiquitous Longines stopwatch. This same watch appears in numerous photos of Virot when he was alive. It's the same timepiece that found itself into Daniel's possession, and which Sophie proudly held up during our Skype conversation.

* * *

Through various newspaper and archive material, I managed to put together a fairly good idea of what happened on Bastille Day in 1957. The day before, Tour debutant Jacques Anquetil – a rider so calculating he was once described as pedalling like an insurance agent – retained the yellow jersey with victory in a 10-kilometre time trial in Barcelona. Having moved into the race lead a week earlier in the Alps, Anquetil carried a four-minute advantage over compatriot Jean Forestier into the Pyrenees. With a second, longer time trial on the horizon, his *maillot jaune* looked increasingly safe. (Such was 19-year-old Anquetil's imperiousness during a time trial in Rouen in 1953 that Virot had questioned on air whether kilometres in Normandy were in fact only 900 metres long.)

Most of France would have tuned in for Sunday's 220-kilometre 'Étape Cinzano', which brought the race back to home soil via the Cols de Tosas and Puymorens on the country's national holiday. With storm clouds looming, Italy's Gastone Nencini, the reigning Giro champion, was among the early attackers foiled by Anquetil before a small break formed. When 27-year-old Frenchman Jean Bourlès rode clear after 60 kilometres, another French regional rider, local favourite Marcel Queheille, set off in pursuit, prompting a response if not by the peloton then by Virot and his driver.

Virot had spent much of his career in cycling precariously perched behind his close friend, Wagner.

'People often ask me why I insist on covering 5,000 kilometres of the Tour on the back of a motorcycle – at an age when you would expect me

to be offered the best comfy chair in the house,'
a newspaper reporting his death quoted Virot as
having once said. 'It's quite simply so that I can
follow all the battles better – to see something that
you cannot see or experience in a car. I am like that.
You can't change your ways.'

One of Sophie's photos shows the duo in action
during the 1952 Critérium du Dauphiné. Wagner, in
a grey boiler suit and shades, looks directly into the
lens while Virot, balancing behind in plus fours and
a sleeveless white shirt, gazes over his right shoulder,
holding a newspaper in one hand and gripping the
back of the saddle with the other. Neither man wears
a helmet – not compulsory until 1973.

If the picture looks like a health and safety nightmare, it's worth adding that Wagner was known
for his equilibrium and excellent safety record: his
first-ever bike crash would be his last.

With the first climb approaching, Virot's voice
was last heard on the radio at 12.30pm. In a tribute
published in *L'Humanité* in 2001, the veteran *Miroir
Sprint* journalist Émile Besson recalled his friend's
final moments.

'The die had been cast, the atmosphere very
calm,' Besson wrote in the article, entitled *Adieu au
Capitaine Alex*. 'Next to us and on his motorbike,
Alex Virot, the great reporter at Radio Luxembourg,
chatted away with his hand clasping our wing mirror.
In front, Bourlès rode clear on his long break. Virot

Virot and Wagner

said to me: "Right, see you later. The Tour is over."
A few hundred metres later we saw a crowd gathered on a slight uphill corner. Virot and his driver
Roger [sic] Wagner were lying in a gully. We descend-
ed quickly, but Virot had died on the spot.'

Perhaps Besson was among the figures at the
scene of the crash in that graphic photo. In the
article, he proceeded to explain that he and Virot had
been in the same anti-Gestapo brigade during the
Resistance before losing contact after the Liberation.

'I used to listen to Virot – one of the first men to
deliver live radio reports from the Tour – but I never
thought it was *Capitaine Alex*.'

It wasn't until Besson started working on the Tour
in 1953 that he realised they were the same person.

Building on Besson's account, there's a separate description of the accident by the last person to see Virot alive: Marcel Queheille, the rider whose tussle with lone leader Bourlès Virot was chronicling at the time.

'The motorbike started to accelerate; then, about 50 metres in front of me, it lost its balance on the gravel and started zigzagging as the riders fought to keep it upright,' he said. 'It hit a road marker, then another, then flew into emptiness. I saw two legs in the air and shoes flying off. Never in my life will I forget that.'

An editorial in Besson's *Miroir Sprint* the next day reported the 'amazement and disbelief' that spread around the *caravane* following the 'stupid accident' which 'engulfed everyone in sadness'.

Virot was the doyen of the press room – a lovable man known as *'bon papa Virot'* by his colleagues.

'How could these two men who had completed ten Tours together die in such a way? The peloton, already warned, didn't seem to understand the commotion as it passed the tragic spot. The Tour continued, for sure, but its spirit was no longer there. Everyone was thinking about Virot and his driver. When they later found themselves in Ax-les-Thermes, squeezed side by side, the radio reporters felt an immense emptiness. In front of the microphone, one of theirs was missing.'

The incident was front page news. In his

memoirs, the journalist Maurice Achard – at the time
a young boy – recalls his despair, claiming it was up
there with the death of his father.

'My half-sister could have died, too, and I would
have been less touched by her death,' he added. The
void left by Virot is apparently still felt today. Writing to her local paper, *Vosges Matin*, on July 3, 2013
(the day Mark Cavendish won the Tour's fifth stage
in Marseille), amateur historian Renée Viard felt an
urge to express her admiration for 'the bees of the
Tour' – the moto men who bring the race to the
people and whose work is often overlooked.

'I remember returning home in a hurry after work
to listen to the "Good evening, dear listeners" of
"bon papa Virot" (I still haven't forgotten his voice).
And then, one evening, the reporter who followed
the Tour with him (his name eludes me, I'm afraid),
in floods of tears, announced the sad news: our *"bon
papa Virot"* had fallen into a ravine with his driver
and we would no longer be able to hear his voice. All
the listeners (for we didn't have television at the time)
were, like me, deeply saddened. Poor *"papa Virot"*
seems to be forgotten now – but not by me. I still
think of him during every Tour stage.'

Victory on Bastille Day should be the crowning
moment of any Frenchman's career, but luckless
Jean Bourlès – who beat Queheille by just over four
minutes – saw his moment of glory overshadowed
by the loss.

'My win was beautiful, but spoiled by the accident,' the Breton would later admit. A minute's silence preceded stage 17. Many riders and journalists wore black ribbons around their arms. An editorial in *Le Monde* spoke of the 'tragic and horrifying' incident which had ended the life of a hugely respected figure. Virot had become 'a victim of his mission to inform' in the 'very dangerous game' that journalists faced on a daily basis while following the race: 'To lose one's life in a sporting spectacle in which one is not even participating is to pay too much.'

Some good came of the tragedy: a reduction in numbers of race motorbikes was introduced in 1958 along with a special Prix Alex Virot awarded to the Tour's most loyal rider. Frenchman Édouard Delberghe was the first to win a prize that ran for a decade alongside a host of other minor gongs, such as luckiest rider, most elegant rider and most pleasant rider. There was even talk, among the Tour's motorbike drivers, of introducing a Prix Wagner for the rider who yielded the most space when being overtaken.

'I am proud when I think of this prize,' Sophie said. 'For me, loyalty means honesty and a loving heart. It's one of the most beautiful values, and proof that my grandfather was clearly a good man with a strong character. He was very passionate, very focused on his goals and very alive – just like my father.'

The two men also sounded very similar, although

this was something Sophie could not yet confirm. Given Virot's celebrity came from his communication with millions of people, it was odd to think that she had never heard her grandfather speak. But he died long before she was born and archive footage of Virot, who worked primarily for private stations, had proved burdensome to track down.

'It would be a huge gift if I could find a recording one day. Hearing his voice would give me a concrete link with him – as if he were actually talking to me. It would make me feel I knew him better. But it would also be very emotional for me because my mother told me that my father and Alex had exactly the same voice.'

Eager to help – and by now genuinely curious to unearth the voice of the man whose life was unravelling before my eyes – I scoured the net. The online database of the Institute National de l'Audiovisuel listed one black-and-white snippet from the 1951 Tour that seemed promising.

Shot from a balcony of an unnamed town in Isère, the amateur footage shows the passing of the peloton after a Cinzano- and Ricard-fuelled *caravane*, conspicuous by its absence of a Suze-swigging miniature accordionist (this was a year before Yvette Horner joined the circus). Ahead of the riders, a clapped-out Renault emblazoned with the Radio Luxembourg logo mounts the kerb and parks. The name 'Alex Virot' is written in capitals underneath a

roof-rack laden with suitcases. A technician gets out
to plug wires into a local phone connection (this was
how early broadcasts were transmitted before the
invention of the satellite).

The whole thing plays out in silence, including the
tantalising short sequence that follows the peloton's
procession: an old man in a white cap, sunglasses
and a spotted cravat (with a leather strap around his
shoulders) speaks methodically into a microphone,
surrounded by eager onlookers. The footage skips
to Virot, cigarette in mouth, clambering onto his
motorbike. Wagner then pulls clear and the pair zip
off to rejoin the action.

Seeing a mute Virot deliver one of his four daily
live Tour packages was encouraging, yet frustrating.
Here was the man now so familiar to me – but
deprived of his distinct calling card: his voice. Even
so, those soundless seconds showed someone very
much in his element. Noted for his level-headedness,
objectivity and precision, Virot was said to have
possessed an uncanny knack of describing to a T his
surroundings and the movements of the peloton. He
was the epicentre of the radio revolution that helped
people discover the noises of the Tour and the
regions it passed through – most famously, the
cicadas of the Midi.

Drawing on his artistic heritage, Virot painted
colourful spoken portraits of riders that were
unmatched by his peers. Recalling his memories of

the Tour as a child, the writer Noel Tulot wrote in *L'Équipe* magazine in 1990: 'For me, cycling was first and foremost a voice – and Virot wrote a sonorous text with his microphone that lay somewhere between the popular novel and an epic.'

Of course, his painstaking precision wasn't to everyone's taste. In his otherwise glowing tribute in *L'Humanité*, Émile Besson admitted that he found his friend's delivery monotonous and measured – especially his revered boxing commentaries.

'His keen eye for detail and meticulous descriptions gave the impression – at least, to me – that the boxers were exchanging punches… every couple of minutes. You can just imagine how that would translate to riders crossing summits or sprinting over the finish line.'

Admitting that he had probably over-egged the pudding, Besson went on to praise 'this very respectable and talented journalist' whose professionalism and opportunism were no better epitomised than in his coverage of the German invasion of Austria in 1938.

Virot's unlikely broadcast of the Nazis entering Vienna was a huge pre-war radio scoop, boasting his distinct blend of ingenuity, resourcefulness and luck. Marcel Bleustein, Virot's boss at Radio-Cité (and founder of advertising giant Publicis), recalls him being in the Swiss resort of Englebert for the skiing world championships at the time. On the instruction of his producer, Virot made his way by train to Vienna where he found the usual lines of communication barred by strict Nazi censorship. Thinking on his feet, he borrowed the phone at a bar as if he were a regular patron. While dictating a live report on what he had witnessed, 'the most unexpected of chances' presented itself.

'In front of my eyes, the first waves of German soldiers marched by,' Bleustein, in his memoirs, reports Virot as saying. 'I opened the cabin and stretched the wire as far as I could so that I could stand by the entrance. I saw the first lines of soldiers entering Vienna and the familiar sounds of their boots could be heard over my report. My idea had succeeded perfectly.'

But it wasn't over yet. By some fluke, Hitler's car – flanked by tanks, motorcycles and a sea of swastikas – stopped 'hardly three metres away. The Chancellor got out and saluted a general right in front of my very eyes'.

And it didn't stop there, either. Having boarded a train to head back to Switzerland, Virot sat alone in the carriage as two German officers entered. According to Bleustein, Virot was still wearing a green cape and a small badger-skin hat procured from the mountains. Perhaps it was the traditional Tyrolean clothes or his detached demeanour – but the Germans felt they were in the presence of an authentic Austrian, and switched to French.

'Now we just need to liquidate the Polish Corridor,' said one. 'It's an intolerable situation and cannot continue. We must do something to sort it out for once and for all.'

We all know what happened next.

Europe's bungled attempts to halt German expansion were also witnessed by Virot, who six months later covered the Munich Crisis, where he ran into the Führer again (as well as Messrs Mussolini, Chamberlain and Daladier – rivalling, perhaps, his previous audiences with King Haile Selassie of Ethiopia and the Pope).

As these escapades revealed themselves to me, I increasingly felt I was dealing with a real-life Forrest Gump figure bent on populating key historical moments of the mid-20th century like a character in a William Boyd novel.

Not content with transmitting a slice of history to his fellow citizens through a bar telephone a few bike lengths away from the most feared moustache of all time, or eavesdropping Nazi generals chatting about carving up Poland, or sitting in as Europe's heads of state tried to avert the inevitable, Virot, as we know, fought for his country on two occasions, juggling his duties of pilot and French *résistant* alongside his busy schedule of commentating on the world's biggest cycling race. While evidence of him trying his hand at shrimp farming, long-distance running or table tennis is lacking, I'd venture that if life

were like a box of chocolates then here was someone
who had already raided all the toffee pennies.

* * *

By all accounts, there was little to suggest from
Virot's early adult life that he would go on to be such
a journalistic colossus. Already aware of his artsy
persuasion, I had no idea his leanings stretched
beyond sketches and sculpture to the stage. But yes,
apparently Virot had been cast in numerous theatri-
cal roles during his 20s. In fact, that mute amateur
coverage of Virot in Isère was not his first (albeit
inadvertent) foray into the genre: he'd previously
been a silent movie star of minor renown. Something
I wouldn't have believed had Sophie not provided
photographic evidence of a boyish Virot on stage
wearing a toga and, looking like a teenage Count
Dracula, cupping a coquettish girl's breast with his
hand (this was from a silent movie and not a stab at
another, more risqué, genre).

Sophie's treasure chest of images allowed me to
fill in the gaps and draw a more complete picture
of the man. There's Virot the soldier smoking in the
trenches and playing cards with fellow servicemen;
Virot the aviator posing in a balaclava and goggles
before take-off; young Virot standing atop a mountain with a rope around his waist; a more worldly wise
Virot relaxing on a chalet balcony (a cross between

debonair Bond villain and a better-looking version of Bob Gunton – the actor who played the crooked prison warden in *The Shawshank Redemption*.)

In one cycling snap he rocks a full-length leather jacket and hugs 1933 Paris-Tours winner Jules Merviel, who, in a written dedication, thanks 'Monsieur Virot' for the 'eulogies and good publicity through the microphone'.

But his traces are more solid than a pile of photos. Originally cast in gilt-bronze in 1909, a second version of Bourdelle's masterpiece, Hercules the Archer, was developed in the sculptor's studio in 1923 while Virot was doing his apprenticeship.

'The model who posed for the sculpture did not want his face to be recognised, so Alex modelled the head of Hercules,' Sophie admitted. 'You can easily see my grandfather in the profile of the statue, which is in the Musée d'Orsay.'

Copies of the cast were also sold to museums in Brussels, Prague, New York, Toyko, Buenos Aires, New Orleans, Dallas, Toulouse, Lyon, Montauban and Egreville. How fitting that there exists vessels the world over of this diminutive man – a pocket Hercules, if you will – who thrived on such insatiable wanderlust.

'He achieved a lot in his career, and successfully tried his hand at practically everything,' Sophie agreed. 'He never stood still, was always moving. He had a strong character and didn't fear anything or anyone. He always lived with his luggage ready at home and a map of the train times in his pocket.'

Such fear of inertia was corroborated by Raymond Marcillac, who described his colleague as 'a man plagued by restlessness. After he had finished running after the facts, he ran after his microphone; once he had his microphone, he ran after his observations, after all those evocative adjectives, and after the riders he wanted to interview'.

Riders were not the only thing Virot chased.

'He was…' Sophie laughed, 'very attractive to women. Not only was he handsome, he also had this free spirit that ensured he lived a very nice life. He never married – he loved women far too much for that. In fact, he always told my father to avoid marriage and just enjoy life.' (Ignoring the advice, his son tied the knot one year after Virot passed away, fathered three daughters and passed his years working in finance in Geneva.)

This reputation as a ladies' man made me consider the not entirely rum possibility that Virot may have tried working the magic with a certain feisty accordionist of similarly limited verticality – one who joined the Tour bandwagon very much in his heyday. Sure, Yvette Horner was married – but such conventions hadn't stopped Virot before…

I needn't have worried. Horner, it turned out, was very much devoted to her husband. They met when she was just 14, and touted for concertinaed

greatness. It was love at first sight – their eyes meeting through a packed crowd at one of the cabaret
clubs she was selling out every night. A few years
later, they married. René Droesch was a footballer
for Girondins de Bordeaux at a time when kicking
a ball was not as lucrative as it is today. He quit,
and they moved to Paris seeking their fortune like a
couple in a Balzac novel.

When Horner joined the Tour *caravane*, René
drove the Citroën upon which she performed (they
later upgraded to a Ford).

'At the finish each day I was all dirty with everything that I had picked up along the road – mos-
quitoes, dust, you name it,' Horner told *L'Équipe* in
2012. 'But how we loved to play! All over France,
children came from their accordion clubs to hear me.
And every evening, we played again. When did we
sleep? We hardly slept at all!'

René eventually designed a protective plexiglass
screen to combat the insects and dust that would
gather in her eyes and mouth (giving Horner's wag-
on something of a papal aspect). But manipulating a
cumbersome instrument weighing 12 kilograms (the
same as a Roubaix cobblestone) for up to five hours
on end, while balancing on a car roof, took its toll.
Salvation came in the form of a life-sized, accordion-
holding, replica waxwork worthy of Madame
Tussauds. Placed strategically on the roof while one
of her records played from a speaker gave the real

Yvette an opportunity to take the odd break from her duties.

After her husband passed away in 1986, Horner dealt with the loss by reinventing herself. As an orange-haired temptress with a predilection for Jean-Paul Gaultier dresses, she marked Gay Pride in 1994 by performing a duet with Boy George. She still plays today, in her tenth decade.

In 2012 – a year before her American namesake Chris became the oldest rider to win a Grand Tour – Horner released her latest album, *Hors Norme* (Out of the Ordinary). Inevitably, the trolls had a field day: 'Yvette Horner's still recording albums in her 90s and her son Chris has won the Vuelta aged 41. *Pas normale*,' one mused.

My attempts to reach Horner and enquire after her memories of the 1957 Tour had fallen on deaf ears. Her agent would not reply to my emails or calls, nor did he accept a barrel-scraping friend request on Facebook.

I'd been harbouring desperate yet faint hopes that Horner might hold the key to identifying the third signee on Colin's Tour road book. At a loose end, I left a message on the *Mémoire du Cyclisme* online forum. Within hours, I struck gold.

'I think (but I'm not sure) that it might be Luc Varenne – the famous Belgian journalist,' came the first reply, corroborated moments later by a second: 'Yes, it is indeed the signature of Luc Varenne – see here.' The attached link was a signed photo of a jowly Varenne advertising a cough sweet called Pectorine (*'Mon bonbon préféré'*) and dedicated to someone called Renée. The signatures were practically identical. What I mistook for a J was an L all along – not that it made much difference: Varenne's was a signature scrawled so frequently it had become a mere nod to the ten letters that justified its existence. Still, it could have been worse: he may have kept his original name…

Born Alphonse Tetaert almost a quarter of a century after Virot, Varenne also had a military background before entering the media – fighting Rommel in Tunisia for the Foreign Legion, then moving to London to help preparations for the D-Day landings.

On leaving Algiers, a woman entrusted Tetaert with a letter for her husband. This Belgian exile in London turned out to be Georges Dumont – the man responsible for overseas Belgian radio broadcasts from the BBC. Dumont required a right-hand man, and fate seemed to have delivered him one. Needing a snappier radio moniker, Alphonse picked the name that would immortalise him from a list of ten suggestions drawn up by a secretary.

After the war, Varenne forged a long and successful career with Radio Télévision Belge Francophone (RTBF), primarily covering football, tennis and cycling. Making his Tour debut in 1948, Varenne quickly established a reputation for lavish picnic

spreads upon car bonnets, a daily whisky *apéritif* and
evening glasses of armagnac. His benign ubiquity
saw him trickle into popular culture: Varenne appeared in the Dutch-language newspaper comic strip
Nero in 1956 in a story entitled The Nine Peppercorns, during which the eponymous anti-hero (with
delicious prescience) discovers in a bunch of African
peppercorns a stimulant that allows him to beast a
Tour mountain stage by 38 minutes. (Coincidentally,
both Varenne and Marc Sleen – Nero's creator –
would receive knighthoods on the same day in 1998.)

The prolific Varenne invigorated radio commentary with a chatty, passionate and highly partisan style
so prized that viewers would mute their TVs and tune
into Varenne instead. For thousands of Belgians, *Le
Soir* remarked, Varenne's voice was something of a
'memory machine', triggering nostalgic pangs akin to
Proust's zesty madeleines.

But if both Virot and Varenne stood out for their
lyrical descriptions, the two were very much belts and
braces when it came to holding up the Tour's trousers. Virot, a stickler for detail, remained objective
to the last; Varenne, who openly admitted to having 'embellished the truth' during his career, had a
subjective streak that bordered on the childish – but
one that enamoured his listeners. Bold, charismat-
ic, opinionated and brash, Varenne was the kind of
commentator that the new cycling business group
Velon would love: he was essentially a bike camera

mounted on Eddy Merckx's Colnago. For shifting
between joy and despair, his emotion and enthusiasm
hit peaks and troughs while on air – and no more
was this clearer than when the subject matter was
Merckx.

'Everything changed the day Eddy Merckx
arrived. He was the joy of my life,' Varenne, doting
husband and a father to two daughters, once said.
If Virot had an illegitimate son in Daniel Olchanski,
then Varenne found the son he never had in
Merckx. From the moment '*mon petit Eddy*' won his
first monument through to his infamous collapse en
route to Pra Loup, Varenne unashamedly planted his
foot in the rider's camp. When Merckx claimed his
sixth Milan-San Remo, such was Varenne's elation
that he lost his balance, fell off his chair and tumbled
off the media scaffold at the finish. When another
Belgian, Roger De Vlaeminck, had pipped Merckx
in the 1970 Liège-Bastogne-Liège, Varenne – whose
love for Merckx dwarfed even his own jingoism –
couldn't suppress a curse on air.

Together, reporter and rider rode a virtual
tandem during the many highs and few lows of The
Cannibal's career. And this wasn't a mere fixation
from the reporter's part: Merckx himself admitted to
falling in love with cycling as a 12 year old because of
Varenne's commentary.

When Luis Ocaña had Merckx on the ropes
during the Pyrenees in 1971, Varenne even swapped

the RTBF car for a motorbike, drew up alongside
Merckx and offered encouragement as if he were his
directeur sportif – all the more unforgettable because
Varenne relayed false information, telling Merckx
that he trailed his rival by five minutes when in fact
the gap was eight.

In his biography of Merckx, Daniel Friebe
mentions how an enraged Varenne – live on air
during the same Tour, when a convoy of vehicles
appeared to be protecting Ocaña from crowds during
a time trial to Albi – implored the Belgian navy to
bomb the French coastline.

'Why shouldn't I have rooted for Merckx?'
Varenne said in an interview during the 90s. 'For 21
years I reported on the success of others – Coppi,
Bobet, Kubler, Koblet, even Anquetil – and then
suddenly Belgium has a star as sensational as
Merckx… Of course I'm going to be Merckxist.
How can anyone reproach me for that?'

He went further, claiming, 'A good commentator must be partisan. There's nothing worse than
someone who is completely neutral. You must let
your heart to the talking. Of course, there were times
when I really put my foot in it – but at least with me
you know exactly where I stand.'

The whole of Belgium knew exactly where
Varenne stood when Merckx attacked on the Col
d'Allos during the 1975 Tour. With Eddy en route
to an unprecedented sixth victory, Varenne gushed

('He's a demon! But a good demon, naturally. What a king! It's unimaginable. I have tears in my eyes!') before handing over the commentary reins ('I'm too emotional!') to his colleague, Georges Malfait.

But by the time Varenne had reached the booth at the finish line in Pra Loup, Bernard Thévenet had turned the race on its head. Merckx had popped, and the Frenchman was riding into yellow. Confused and shocked, Varenne learned this only as he returned on air.

'What? Eddy Merckx has been caught? It's not true! What are you talking about, Georges? It can't be. That is terrible. Unimaginable. My breath has been taken away. It's the worst day in my entire life. Oh-la-la! Poor Eddy. Poor Eddy… And poor us! He was flying towards victory. No one could have seen that coming. He was the hero. My God, what a dream – and what a nightmare, too.' (This is merely an edited version.)

Reflecting on the dark day shortly before he passed away in 2002, Varenne channelled Prince Philip by admitting that he'd 'have willingly been Japanese rather than experience what I was suffering that day'.

'There are two spectacles on the Tour de France,' RTBF's other fabled voice, Armand Bachelier, once said. 'That of Eddy Merckx – calm, serene, pedalling with tranquility – and that of Luc Varenne: a volcano in permanent eruption.'

* * *

It's impossible to tell whether or not Anquetil could have been to Virot what Merckx was to Varenne. Virot's death just one week before the first of Anquetil's five wins perhaps deprived French listeners of the kind of rider-reporter double-act soon to be enjoyed by their Belgian counterparts.

A year after he passed, the first live TV images recorded during a Tour stage were somewhat symbolically broadcast from the summit of the Aubisque – the same mountain where Virot had made that ground-breaking radio report 26 years earlier. Virot had made his debut for Télé Luxembourg while covering the Six Jours de Paris in 1956, but the TV revolution came a bit too late in his career – and life. Varenne himself was 64 – three years younger than Virot at the time of his death – when he covered his 30th and final Tour in 1978. It's often said that the emergence of television called time on Varenne's career – not least because fans could now see how a goal attempt that supposedly grazed the post in fact went some ten metres wide of the mark.

For all their similarities and differences, Virot and Varenne marked a dying breed of journalist whose depictions of the events became, for their listeners, the events themselves. It's fitting, even touching, that by some quirk of fortune their signatures, alongside Yvette Horner's, ended up on the front cover of that media pack. Between them, these personalities notched 63 Tours while becoming very much part of the race furniture. And yet I'd venture that, like me, most readers of *The Cycling Anthology* were previously unaware of both reporters, if not the accordionist who provided the *caravane*'s soundtrack for more than a decade.

While Varenne's frenzied delivery and Horner's wistful chords can be revived at the click of a mouse, the oeuvre of their pioneering Tour predecessor – arguably more accomplished, radical and important – seemed to have been lost. My efforts to track down archive material and help Sophie finally hear her grandfather's voice had fallen flat. Dishearteningly, the closest I'd got was that agonisingly mute video of Virot in action. I had learnt so much about a man whose bafflingly dormant personal history seemed at odds with his dazzling achievements. The tongue responsible for popularising the Tour had by some calamity been posthumously removed. All I could give Sophie were a few words instead from the man who runs the Tour today.

'Alex Virot was a great witness of the Tour: by plane or by motorbike, he was one of those who created and wrote the legend,' Christian Prudhomme said. 'The Tour is what it is today thanks to people like him, who put words on the race and described the story of its champions. The Tour is an invention of journalists, created by the written press and popularised by the radio – and Alex Virot was one of radio's first stars. He had a great talent of gauging the atmosphere and bringing the race alive for those who couldn't be there. He tragically "died on stage" – like Molière, as we say in France – on the day of the French national holiday. But he will definitely remain an important narrator of the Tour de France story.'

A narrator who regretfully no longer appeared to have a voice.

That was, until the email from Luxembourg's Centre National de l'Audiovisuel dropped into my inbox. The CNA had previously stressed that its only archive material of Virot was a non-speaking cameo in a documentary. But then, out of the blue, my contact pinged over a two-minute clip with the header: 'I have found his voice!'

With butterflies in my stomach, I clicked on the download. A black-and-white photo montage of Virot accompanied by a crackly radio report whirred into life.

'Radio Luxembourg listeners, good morning. As you can hear from the loudspeaker, we are deep in the theatrics of the sign-on before today's stage. Here we are in the Place de Catalogne and the people of Barcelona have got up bright and early – which is not normal, I tell you. They must really love the Tour to have come to see the start at this hour.'

Blimey, it wasn't just Virot's voice – it was his final pre-stage broadcast.

'Now, we're going to try and speak to some riders and see how they spent the night. Ah, perfect timing – here's Jean Bobet... How's your sore finger?'

'It's much better,' says Bobet, the less illustrious younger brother of triple Tour winner Louison. 'I'm lucky – we've managed to stem the pain. It's still not perfect, but it's okay.'

'Good – so your battle with [Fernand] Picot can resume?'

'Yes, indeed. With Picot and [Marcel] Rohrbach.'

'Oh yes, of course!'

(Bobet, Rohrbach and Picot were currently the best-placed French *régionals* in a race utterly dominated by Anquetil's national team. Bourlès's victory that afternoon would be only the third for a *régional* rider, against 17 for the national team.)

'My target is still to be the best *régional*,' Bobet admits.

'And it's a beautiful ambition.'

'We've really been forced to make do with the scraps thanks to the superiority of the French national team...'

'Yes, they're running away with everything. They are *terrible*' [terrific]!

'Well, they're obviously very strong.'

'They're strong, of course, but they're also extremely greedy,' jokes Virot – a nod, perhaps, to Champagne-and-oyster-guzzling Anquetil, the consummate gourmand.

'Good for them,' says Bobet. 'It's just a pity for us.'

'But don't they have indigestion?'

Bobet laughs. 'Maybe they will!'

Effortlessly affable, Virot suggests that Bobet has shown enough promise to earn a place in the national team. In turn, Bobet vows to fight until Paris. (The call-up would never come: Bobet's second Tour would be his last.)

The clip ends with Virot thanking the rider with a magnanimous double *merci*.

I called Sophie on Skype and sent over the file, keeping shtum about its contents. I wanted to witness her reaction as her dream to hear Virot's voice was finally realised.

'What's this – a movie?'

The clip started. At first, confusion; then, a smile.

'It's Alex? *Non*! It's incredible!' Sophie's hands came up to her face in astonishment. 'Thank you so much. It's perfect. What a surprise! What a huge gift.'

She was almost as ecstatic as Varenne commentating a Merckx victory.

'You know what?' she said later. 'It's not exactly the same voice as my father – but there's something in their way of speaking that's so similar. It's very moving to hear. I can't thank you enough.

'Alex has become so much a part of my life – I'm surrounded by his stuff, his art, his photos. Now I really feel like he's living with me.'

* * *

What's that saying about waiting for buses? Well, the next morning I received an audio file from a historian at RTL (formerly Radio Luxembourg) who had earlier warned me that the chances of locating anything were as slight as Alejandro Valverde. Yet here was a full ten minutes from the same broadcast as the Bobet snippet.

Between 9am and 9.40am on Sunday, July 14 1957 – as the riders gathered ahead of the stage 16 start – Alex Virot had been a busy bee. Like Martin Brundle on the Formula One grid, he was obviously an avowed part of the pre-race hype. Hearing him shoot the breeze with the race protagonists was confirmation of the man's popularity and passion. Peppering his easy flow of informal, informative chatter, and his avuncular tutelage of the French youngsters, Virot's propensity for cheery badinage exposed a lighter side to his personality.

Always employing the informal '*tu*', Virot dances from rider to rider, all of whom seem very happy to share their thoughts. He greets with gusto Frenchman Nicolas Barone – the yellow jersey for one day during the opening week – with a '*Voilà, le seigneur!*'

Playing this down ('*Le seigneur ne va pas bien!*' – the lord is not doing so well), Barone opens up about a stomach ache and a previous crash. 'I'm a bit paralysed,' he admits. 'I hope I'll make it to Paris.'

'But of course you will. Not only that – you should try your luck in the mountains.'

'Yes, but I've never appeared before the people of Paris so my priority is to at least finish the Tour.'

'*Très bien, mon petit Barone.* I hope – and I'm sure – that you'll do well. Ruby…!'

And he's off to quiz Pierre Ruby about whether the race was harder the year before ('Hmm. It's about the same'). They talk about the high average speed, the heat and looming rain clouds before Virot accosts a journalist for his thoughts on the Pyrenees. Virot agrees that today's stage is the easiest of the three, but adds the caveat: 'It's a bit unknown. No one is familiar with the profile and so it's hard to make any predictions.'

Then there's an amusing section with a bunch of Belgian riders, who Virot cannot initially reach because his route is cut off by a procession of sorts.

'Hurry up, please, we're trying to work!' he says, raising his voice in a rare flash of disgruntlement before returning to his schoolmasterly self, gently ribbing the slightly dour Flemish talent Marcel Janssens for putting the Alps and the Pyrenees 'in the same basket'. ('You really think they're the same because the road goes uphill in both?')

Virot's last interviewee is Jozef Planckaert, who says his focus is more on tomorrow's stage. Sheer bluff: Planckaert gets in the breakaway that Virot soon follows on the back of Wagner's motorcycle.

And some four hours after the pair plummet to their deaths, it's Planckaert who finishes fourth in Ax-les-Thermes.

Having no doubt consulted the same stage time-table that appears in Colin's 1957 road book, Virot knows exactly what time the stage was scheduled to finish. He now just needs to bid adieu to those listeners having their Bastille Day breakfasts, before scuttling off to watch the start.

'*Alors…* Listeners of Radio Luxembourg, I will see you for our programme at the arrival of today's stage, which should take place around 4.27pm – of course, provided we're not delayed in any way. *Bon appétit!*'

- FIN -

Felix Lowe has covered the Grand Tours and major Classics for Eurosport's website for the past decade. He blogs (Blazin' Saddles), tweets (@saddleblaze) and writes *Cyclist* magazine's Last Gasp column. His first book – *Climbs and Punishment: Riding to Rome in the Footsteps of Hannibal* – was published in June 2014.

8

With the scourge that was doping swiftly eradicated from professional sport in 2017, a number of athletes have been busily looking for new ways to boost their incomes.

And one such rider – codename Lapin – knows all the tricks of the pro-cycling trade, writes **Ellis Bacon**.

LAPIN

BY ELLIS BACON

In the shadows of the far end of an almost-empty car park, around the back of a budget hotel chain on the outskirts of Ghent, Lapin was waiting for his cut of the money, and further instructions.

He was of medium height, and weathered and skinny and swarthy. Years of relentless southern European sun, soaked up while racing and training, had turned him into an identikit pro bike rider. He wasn't even European, but had come here as a young man, and, save for a short stint living and racing in Belgium in his teens in the early 2000s, had made France home.

Now, married to a French woman and with three half-French – but basically wholly French – children, he wasn't likely to ever leave.

If he wasn't a pro rider, Lapin would have grimly lit, and as equally grimly smoked, a cigarette as he stood, shivering, in the darkness. Instead, he up-turned his mouth against the now-falling drizzle and cursed the man he was still waiting for. It was 10pm, for God's sake. He should be in bed by now.

* * *

'Lapin' was the name of his daughter's rabbit – in French, of course. It was a case of that childish obsession with calling, say, a toy cat Cat. But it was lazy, and simply lacked imagination, thought Lapin.

'If I can call my teddy bear Teddy, why can't I call my rabbit Lapin?' she'd reasoned – in perfect French. It wasn't Lapin's first language, of course, but, outside of the circus that was the pro peloton, it was pretty much the only language he ever spoke these days.

And 'Lapin' made for a good codename – as good as anything else. Not that many people even needed him to have a codename; just the man he was waiting for, and that man's bosses – a Bermudian gang, maybe; Lapin didn't really know. He laughed as he thought about it, waiting. Bermudian? Like he knew what a Bermudian accent sounded like. Whatever – they had accents that were a combination of an Eton education and holidays spent on a beach in paradise, Lapin decided. Yeah – something like Bermudian.

While his team-mates had often partaken in similarly nefarious-looking meetings in the past to get hold of, or pay for, their dope, Lapin was relatively relaxed for what was just another meeting to get the money he was owed and the information for the next bet. As long as the guy turned up soon. If not, everything was going to have to be rearranged, and that was just going to be a pain in the arse rather than anything more serious.

Lapin had made it into one of the world's top-tier teams through a combination of experience as to how this whole world worked, and downright arseholery. Each team had their nice guy and their successful guy – not always one and the same person, but sometimes – and they were the ones the media fawned over and asked questions to in the press conferences. Most of the rest of the team roster went about their business with not a sniff of interest from fans or media. Look at the blokes at either end of any team press-conference line-up; they're there, but no one ever asks them a question. Lapin was one of those, and it was just the way he liked it.

No one gave the tiniest shit, therefore, where he finished in the bunch, and that was the beauty of the scam: 134th or 135th was neither here nor there, but if he could let his equal number on another team beat him, then there was money to be made far beyond what he was earning, which was equal to the equivalent of a crap lawyer.

Teams were always going to give him a job, for as long as he could keep pace. Lapin was a 'fixer' – the type of rider who made things happen, be that in the racing sense, or whatever the team required. A younger rider or a member of staff needed disciplining for some indiscretion or other? The likes of Lapin were your men: invaluable, been-there-done-

it-all types who ruled the peloton through a combination of fear, manic humour and stony silence.

Just then, an almost laughably stereotypical silver
Mercedes pulled up on the other side of the car-park
fence, the driver's-side window whirred open, and a
man's arm extended through the open window and
his fingers through the wire fence.

'Take this,' he said to Lapin.

This was no ampoule, like it might once have
been; it was a roll of paper on which was written,
simply, '[Name] to beat you.' Nothing coded – just
clear instruction. If ever he didn't know the rider's
name on the note, Lapin would look up his race
number the next morning and make sure he then
knew damn well who he was.

Lapin memorised the name, screwed the piece of
paper up, and posted the little ball through the drain
cover beneath his feet.

Next, squeezed through the fence, came an
envelope of cash – thousands of euros – which Lapin swiftly pocketed. He'd count it later; it was always
correct.

The man in the car grunted and shrugged at the
same time. Lapin sniffed, and they parted. Message
received.

* * *

They're called match bets. To make a bet, you choose

who will finish first out of two specified riders. On a mountain stage of a race, a good climber pitched against a less-good climber will have the shortest odds, but the reality is that the match-ups can be very hard to call, especially on flatter stages and when the names involved – names like Lapin's – are somewhat lesser known. Naming the actual outright winner of, say, a stage is, while tough to call, more straightforward, and the more popular choice when betting on bike racing. But the lesser known, almost more hidden, match bets had become the domain of the experts and, these days, the fraudsters.

Doctoring the outcome by involving one of the two riders concerned was not only sporting fraud, but fraud-fraud – fraud proper – and therefore carried the risk not only of a suspension by cycling's world governing body, but also of jail time.

Lapin had no interest in going to prison in the name of sport, and so was extremely careful. In this instance, he'd been talking to the rider whose name appeared on the piece of paper just a couple of days ago, asking him about his new house and his latest girlfriend. The usual. In some ways it made getting the job done even easier. If he dared, Lapin could ride across the line next to the rider, chatting in the closing stages of the race, well off the pace of their leaders, who would have battled it out for the win some minutes before, and just ensure he was half a wheel length behind.

Otherwise, carrying out the job was almost always relatively easy: find the rider, drop to the back of the group, have something to eat, perhaps get some new bottles for his team-mates if he was at the back for too long, distribute them, then let himself drift back once more, all the while keeping track of where the other rider was. Dropping off the pace completely to make double-sure of being beaten was never clever due to the often-strict time limits, but keeping to the back of the group and fighting to stay on their wheel – usually a very real fight in the closing kilometres – was do-able. If his 'rival' couldn't keep pace, it was no problem to be one of the riders who was struggling just as much.

Anyone might have expected the odd slip-up, and the winnings would cancel those out, but it never happened. Despite the risk of untimely punctures or crashes that could have spat the 'target' out of the back of the bunch quicker than a happy baby's dummy just didn't happen. Lapin could locate his rider, hang around with him, follow him – whatever – and then ensure he let him beat him.

In Lapin's world of fraud, and until he got caught, the rewards were always the same: 50 per cent for him, and 50 per cent for... the others. The Bermudians. Whoever they were. It didn't matter.

The amount Lapin received each time – that 50 per cent cut – grew and grew as they became more confident in Lapin delivering, and the messenger was soon even able to tell him in advance roughly how much he could expect to receive from each bet.

And Lapin wasn't in the slightest bit interested in gambling of any kind; the only gamble he took was the risk of getting caught, and there was minimal risk of that.

At least, that's what he thought.

* * *

Pure, green-eyed jealousy had made him do it. Let's call this rider Smith. In fact, that was his real name. He'd heard about Lapin and the others, and what they did. The drugs no longer worked, and Smith was one of the riders who'd had to go back to earning minimum wage, working in the service of others, slogging his guts out every day for meagre reward. Why should Lapin swan about the bunch dishing out justice as the bully that he was, basically doing whatever he wanted, and then take home the kind of money reserved for the sport's top stars?

For 2019, the world governing body had promised to crack down on what it saw as the biggest threat to professional cycling's survival since the doping years. Now, Smith could be a part of helping to save the sport that each and every one of them said they loved so much – by snitching on Lapin and the others.

But where would that get him? Perhaps it was a

case of instead applying that old rule: if you can't beat them, join them.

Initially unaware of the shadowy organisation that Lapin worked with, Smith put money on – who else? – Lapin to beat him in a match bet in the next race they were doing together. There was a delicious irony in this, he grinned, and hung about at the back of the race, where Lapin could normally be found, no doubt busy letting someone else beat him. And when Lapin crossed the line, Smith ensured he finished just behind, and the free money was his. He felt gloriously smug.

The whole process seemed far too easy, just as Lapin had found, and suddenly Smith could see why so many riders did it. The danger, of course, was that the more people who did it, the bigger the chance that the whole pro peloton would turn into one giant slow bicycle race as everyone tried to let everyone else finish before them:

'After you.'

'No, no – after you. I insist.'

And the Bermudians were never going to let that happen.

So as Smith's rewards for match-betting grew, one of his supposed mates put him in touch with who were considered 'the right people' to help him earn the really big money, and when the silver Mercedes pulled up alongside Smith at the traffic lights, on the corner where he always stopped for a coffee on his easier training rides, just outside Monte Carlo, the piece of paper handed to him by the long arm through the open window was a sharp reminder as to why he should have just stayed out of it: 'Lapin to beat you.'

Paranoia took hold of Smith, kept squeezing, and wouldn't let go. Of all the riders, how could it be Lapin? The colour drained from Smith's face. They were on to him, weren't they? There was no other explanation. Someone, somewhere, stood to lose a not-inconsiderable amount of money if he couldn't deliver. What would the consequences be for failing to get the job done? Smith wasn't prepared to find out, so felt he had no choice but to go through with it. But then that would be it. He still had a career of sorts; he'd accept his lot, earn the small salary and, in a few years' time, retire and do something else, with only the guilt of his drug-taking years for company, pushed to the back of his mind. He'd still be a hero to his family and friends, and to all those fans in his hometown. He was a professional cyclist! He'd made it. He was a success.

* * *

On the day of the race – and of the 'Lapin to beat Smith' match bet – Lapin was his usual self, flitting about the bunch, laughing and joking. But beating Lapin should be very do-able if Smith claimed he was feeling unwell, and therefore unable to work for his team's sprinter in the final few kilometres of the race. With no sprinter of note on Lapin's team, he was almost always in the second half of the bunch. If Smith could just keep an eye on Lapin – no one else – this could be over and done with, and things could go back to normal.

But if the colour had drained from our rider's face when he'd seen that he'd been pitched against Lapin in his match bet, try to imagine the colour Smith turned when, with two kilometres to go, Lapin raised his hand

to indicate a puncture.

Smith's immediate, panicked reaction was to throw himself to the ground – one of the most ridiculous attempts at a crash ever seen. He kind of toppled sideways, somehow killing most of his forward motion. It wasn't too dissimilar to a slightly higher-speed version of someone using clipless pedals for the first time and toppling over at the traffic lights when they forgot to disengage their foot in time.

But he was quickly helped to his feet and back onto his bike by members of the public, while Lapin, whose own team car was nowhere to be seen, threw his wheel onto the grass verge, hamming up his frustration at being unable to get mechanical assistance for the watching cameras.

And which rider did 'win', after all? It's irrelevant,

because Smith's farcical theatricals simply helped confirm what the police by then already knew. He was arrested soon after he crossed the finish line and, still in his kit, barely half an hour after finishing the stage, he was being grilled at a nearby police station.

The police were waiting for all of them – Lapin, too.

* * *

From a police perspective, there was absolutely no evidence to link Lapin with the match-betting scandal. None. But, unlike Lapin – who always, always dealt in cash, coupled with the well-stretched side pocket of an old rucksack – Smith should have known better than to use his real name, and to have started out by having the money he won paid straight into his bank account; the police check of every pro rider's account soon showed up the betting companies. It was a big, stupid, rookie mistake.

Smith escaped with a suspended jail sentence and a four-year ban from the sport. Collaborating with the governing body, who launched a major investigation, could have seen his ban reduced, and he would have been able to return to the sport in, perhaps, two years. But the damage was done – all self-inflicted – and his love for the sport was gone. Besides, which team in their right mind would want to re-employ this kind of cheat?

The shame – coupled with the indignity of returning to work in a factory in the town where he'd grown up – gradually crept up on Smith, little by little, until one day it became too much. Eleven years into retirement, Smith stopped his car on the Millau Viaduct, climbed up onto the railings and threw himself off, which got him a few lines in French sports newspaper *L'Equipe*. Fame at last.

A toy rabbit was laid among the flowers by the bridge, which was either a lovely, loving gesture, or someone's idea of a sick joke, Smith thought. Or would have done.

* * *

Things weren't what they used to be in the pro peloton, Lapin thought to himself. It used to be a family – a family in which the darkest secrets would remain safe from prying, outside eyes, and everyone was free to go about earning a living in whichever way they saw fit.

Lapin had been named, and very nearly shamed, in the betting investigation, and everyone knew he was somehow involved. But a lack of evidence had saved him. For the sake of appearances, he was the subject of a separate investigation by his own national cycling federation. But why would anyone want to punish a member of their own family? It helped, too, that one of his sisters-in-law worked for the federation, so it was genuinely family, and he was basically untouchable. How many times had he helped them out anyway, when it had come to helping sort out various issues when it came to the world championships and the Olympics? He was almost as much of a fixer for his national federation as he was for his own trade team.

Sure enough, 'We have no reason to believe that Lapin [except they used his real name] had any knowledge... [etc.]' read the subsequent press release. The press could ask for a comment from Lapin all they liked; the federation and team press officers would fob them off, and no one had Lapin's number. Same old story.

But after that, Lapin was a lot more careful. He reduced the frequency of the match betting, and, with retirement rapidly approaching, soon gave up earning his extra pocket money altogether – happy to see out the last couple of years of his career enjoying his racing, and helping his younger team-mates to forge a clean, honest career for themselves.

And besides, Lapin reminded himself with a smile, no one was ever going to find his bike's hidden motor.

Ellis Bacon is the author of several cycling books, including Mapping Le Tour (Collins) and Great British Cycling (Bantam Press). The latter was shortlisted for the cycling category at the 2015 British Sports Book Awards. He is co-editor of The Cycling Anthology, and, once he's completed the dangerous-fauna therapy, is off to live in Melbourne.

9

Everyone knows Greg LeMond won the 1989 Tour de France, the closest edition of the race ever.

But the drama that happened on the bike was matched by what was going on behind the scenes.

For the first time, **Kathy LeMond** writes about what it was like to support her husband during some of his bleakest days while she was also coping with some potentially devastating news.

This story shows there's often more to a rider's life than the struggle we see on the roads.

BESIDE THE YELLOW JERSEY

BY KATHY LEMOND

For more than 35 years, I have had a hard-won intimacy with the harrowing, exhilarating, punishing sport of professional cycling. Most fans, trainers, and sponsors are keyed into the riders' performances. Each part of the race is thrilling to me. In a way, I get 'hooked', the way other people get obsessive about soap operas. I want to know about the racers' lives, about who they really are. I think the sport is much more fascinating when you know the back stories of the riders. I know from experience that there's a whole person there who is so much more than 'just' a racer; beyond the stats and records is a human being, he is the sum of all of his parts. Often, there are riders in the peloton who are coping with stresses far beyond the physical demands of the race.

For the past couple of years, I have followed the Tour de France inside the ropes because my husband, Greg LeMond, was working as an expert commentator for Eurosport.

Being behind the scenes, close to the finishing straight, mixing with the television producers and journalists and all the other people working on the Tour showed me another side of the race that was very different to the one I followed when Greg was racing for the yellow jersey in the 1980s. Back then, I was on the outside. I drove my car and followed the race like a fan. I'd get to the bottom of a climb like Alpe d'Huez and have to plead with the police to let me drive up. I'd say, 'I'm Kathy LeMond, my husband is Greg LeMond,' and most of the time they would let me pass. But I was never under any illusion that Greg's team wanted me around. The attitude at the time was that wives had no place at the Tour de France.

I admit I got a kick out of my Tour credentials this year because I was identified as an expert. But if I'm an expert in anything, it has everything to do with supporting my husband throughout his career. Perhaps, to a small extent, it may have to do with the fact that I was privy to this astonishing man, and to the lives of professional cyclists.

Greg's historic achievements are Greg's. I was not one of the wives and girlfriends (WAGs) who said: 'Oh, we did so well today! We won the stage! We're wearing the yellow jersey!' No – it was not my performance. I would never, ever be comfortable grabbing credit for his triumphs, or trying to claim some of his genius on a bicycle. But I will say this: I believe with all my heart that my contributions to Greg's well-being helped him to fully inhabit his athleticism and determination.

For 15 years, our lives were completely built around professional cycling. We lived every minute of those years together, searching for times when we could be together in an era when women were not welcome at professional races. The Tour de France is probably the most gruelling endurance sport in the world, likened to running a marathon every day for three weeks. Well, I am here to tell you that the Tour is an endurance sport for the wives and families of riders, too.

I wonder if fans appreciate how much a rider's personal life can affect his ability to perform. It stands to reason that a man who is happy, healthy, settled, and secure will be better equipped to cope with the stress of racing. I have had unusually close proximity to this sport. I know that professional cycling demands almost all of a rider's physical and emotional energy to the point that there is very little left for anything else. And I mean anything else! Most cyclists won't break their rigorous training to do so much as walk around a block. They won't disturb strict training by wasting their precious energy doing chores, child care, or going to the grocery store.

There's a sense that these guys become automatons when they begin a race, and in a way, that's true. But if the cyclist has concerns in his personal life, it surely compromises his ability to give everything he has to racing.

I remember so clearly how I felt in 1989 when

it looked like the stresses on Greg would bring his career to an abrupt, untimely close. He was in deep trouble even before he got to the Giro d'Italia, precursor to the Tour de France. His team-mates, coaches, and fans were frustrated and pained to see that Greg's performance was falling short. Would he ever be the cyclist he used to be – the guy who had won the 1986 Tour?

Neither Greg nor I have ever really spoken fully about the 1989 season, about the reasons for Greg's poor showing in the first half of the year. I especially want to do that now. I think it's important for fans to understand all the elements that affect the riders, and Greg's '89 season may be a helpful example of this.

Greg had been through such a gruesome time recovering from his near-fatal gunshot wounds, received in a hunting accident in the spring of 1987. His battle to survive, and then to return to the sport he loved, was one of the hardest experiences we had been through together.

Honestly, the whole thing was so miraculous. The story of his comeback still has the power to bring me to tears. No professional athlete we had heard of had ever come back to competition after such a horrendous injury. Greg was able to defy all of the odds, to silence his harshest critics, and get back to the joy of racing.

But in the spring of 1989, other stressors were at play.

I was pregnant with our third child, happy that this baby was going to be born in America after the season. I always worried a bit that my pregnancies might 'interfere' with racing, but this one seemed perfectly timed. I was concerned, though, about my husband. He seemed a bit fragile to me while we were still at home in Minnesota. The endless training and pressure appeared to be taking an unusual toll on Greg, emotionally and physically. We talked about it often, and recommitted to the summer season ahead of us.

Greg flew to Italy one morning in May for the Giro, and I was to fly back to our home in Belgium with our two sons, Geoffrey and Scott, later that afternoon. I had recently had an appointment with my obstetrician, and at about four and a half months into this pregnancy, I felt great.

I had packed for the trip and was just having lunch when my doctor called.

'Thank God I've caught you,' he said, his tone grave. 'There's a problem with those blood tests we did. You can't get on a plane today, Kathy. You've got to come back now for further testing.'

I was so devastated I could hardly think. My husband was in the air on his way to Italy, expecting to be able to reach me on the phone that night at our home in Belgium. Our children were the most important part of our life, and now I was hearing that the new baby might be in trouble. We had no cell phones then, and there was no way for me to talk to Greg until that night. I don't know how I managed the terror I was feeling. Naturally, I wanted my husband with me – his strong arms around me, his loving reassurances – and I couldn't have him.

I went to the hospital, where my doctor informed me that the earlier tests indicated the need for amniocentesis. (This is the sampling of amniotic fluid using a hollow needle inserted into the uterus, to screen for developmental abnormalities in a foetus.) After some consultation, the doctors thought the baby had a neural tube defect. The possible disabilities indicated ranged from Down syndrome to spina bifida, a congenital defect of the spine in which part of the spinal cord and its meninges are exposed through a gap in the backbone, often causing paralysis of the lower limbs, and sometimes mental handicap.

There was even a chance I might lose the baby, because one of the potential side effects of the amniocentesis test itself is miscarriage. After the test, I would have to stay an additional 14 days in Minnesota, waiting for the results while Greg raced the Giro.

There would be no afternoon flight to Belgium for me.

I went home.

That night, Greg called from Italy. He'd been ringing our house in Belgium, and was obviously worried because there hadn't been an answer.

Now I had a dilemma. I knew Greg was filled with trepidation about starting the Giro.

He knew it was going to be a very hard race, and, despite all his efforts, his performance just wasn't where it needed to be. He hadn't been riding well, and was so discouraged. I had to tell him why I hadn't made it to Belgium, but I didn't want to worry him too much. I certainly didn't want him to leave the Giro before it even started. Masking my own fears, I gently explained that the doctors were worried about the baby, that there was a chance something might be wrong.

I said I needed to stay in Minnesota to wait for some test results. I didn't go into too many details, and told him how much I wanted him to stay at the race. And I did! I knew how much of his identity was bound up in having a strong season.

Almost unbelievably, our pain increased. My dear cousin, Geoff Brewer, was a stuntman in Hollywood. He was killed in an accident on a movie shoot, leaving behind his wife and child. My mother, who had come from my hometown in Wisconsin to be with me while I awaited the test results, was heartbroken by grief. Geoff had been killed on his father's birthday. Mom mourned so terribly for her brother, his wife, and their loss. I, too, was nearly overcome with sadness.

Emotionally, I went right back to the day in 1987 when, arriving in panic at UC Davis Medical Center, the only thing the doctors could tell me about Greg's condition after the shooting was, 'He's alive right now, but it doesn't look good.'

Far across the Atlantic, Greg was struggling through the beginning of the Giro.

'It was just so hard,' he says. 'There were some long, long stages, and I was getting dropped right from the start. The second stage went to Mount Etna, and I was losing time as soon as we started climbing. The pressure I was putting on myself was ridiculous. My allergies were horrible, affecting my breathing as badly as any 'flu. Our team hadn't been getting paid, and the guys expected me, as their leader, to stand up to management and insist they make good on their promises. Worse, I knew Kathy wasn't telling me everything about what was going on at home. It was all eating at me. I wanted so much to go home to be with her.'

Greg phoned me every night, waiting in line with all the other riders for a chance to use the hotel lobby pay phones as the race progressed from place to place. We talked through his every move, his debilitating allergies, and his bitter discouragement. He talked over and over about how tired he was. I fought the urge to tell him that I was lonely and scared. Instead, I assured him that the boys and I missed him and loved him, and would be on our way to him the minute the doctors cleared me for travel. (Despite my mom's grief, she remained by my side.

She has always loved Greg as a son, and backed my
approach to this all the way. I really don't know what
I would have done without her!)

Then one night came the call I will never forget.

'Honey, I just want to quit,' Greg said.

I believed him. I had never heard such resigna-
tion from him, such defeatism. An athlete of Greg's
calibre isn't necessarily satisfied or grateful that he
had come this far again after the accident that almost
killed him. He wanted to win. Greg simply could not
visualise himself winning the Giro d'Italia, not to
mention the race that came next – the 1989 Tour de
France.

I knew I had to encourage Greg to stay with it,
for his sake.

'Would you feel okay if you quit?' I asked. 'Are
you sure you've given this everything you have? If
you were to quit right now, would you regret it later?'

We talked it over. Finally, I said: 'Listen, honey,
if you can, why don't you stick it out now and quit
at the end of the year? Give your all until the end of
the season, and if you want to stop then, you'll have
no regrets.'

I meant what I said, and Greg knew I meant what
I said. He was suffering, and I wanted to help him. It
seemed that simple to me.

We were so close, so mutually invested in his
well-being. What truly mattered to us was our
marriage and our family. At very young ages, we had

come through some of the hardest challenges a family could face. We knew what really mattered in life. As long as we were all healthy and together, nothing could break us. We could make it through anything. Greg trusted me as completely as I trusted him.

Greg remembers: 'Kathy giving me "permission" to stop was more important to me than anything else. It immediately relieved the pressure on me, because I believed her when she assured me that I could quit, or stay, or do whatever I chose, and we would still be all right.

'That phone call changed the way I was thinking. We had these dreams and hopes as a couple. I felt a great obligation to perform, to secure our financial future. I'd been well on my way to doing that, and then I got shot. I hadn't let that stop me, but there I was, considering quitting mid-race. How would our life go on? What would our future look like? I was a bike racer – if I weren't that any more, who would I be? Kathy and I loved each other. I knew she would always be there for me. I just hadn't been able to see around the obstacles in my way.'

Greg made the decision to stay.

I was so proud of him.

I was a little proud of me, too. Still, I agonised through those 14 days at home. I was worried about my baby, my husband, and about money. We hadn't had any income yet that year. Greg was not getting paid by his ADR team. I was longing to get to the

Giro to comfort and support Greg. I'd been having some contractions since the amniocentesis; finally, they eased.

At last we got the results of the amnio. I can't tell you how happy I was that our baby was fine! (She continued to grow, perfectly healthy, into our beautiful daughter Simone.)

Now I could turn my full attention to Greg. There was no way I'd be content with going home to Belgium; I needed to be with Greg. I booked a flight to Italy and boarded with my two little boys, aged four and two. I was so eager to get there! I was practically counting the miles as we got closer to our goal. When we landed, I rented a little car and drove up into the mountains to find my husband.

I finally got to the crummy little hotel where the team was staying. I remember the moment Greg walked into the lobby, wet through, frozen, and utterly miserable. It was so cold!

I knew he had lost a lot of time on that day's climbing stage, and his face told me everything else I needed to know: he was hurting.

Remember, this was a time before WAGs were permitted to accompany their men. Jose De Cauwer, the *directeur sportif* of Greg's team, was fantastic. He opened up to me and the boys and made no effort to stop Greg from seeing us. I think he realised that Greg's morale couldn't get any lower, and that keeping us apart wasn't going to do him any good.

Greg helped to break down the barriers against women that existed in the sport. He was fed up with me being on the outside all the time. Later that summer, a couple of days before the end of the Tour, he insisted that I be allowed to be with him at the finish of the final stage. He told the officials: 'If I win this thing, I won't get on the podium unless you let my famiily have access to the finish line.' My years of hanging around like some kind of groupie were over.

As wonderful as it was to be reunited with Greg at the Giro, we still had very little hope for success. Greg was depressed. I knew how much of himself he put into cycling, and how much we had both sacrificed to allow him to compete at his best. Any human being can only handle so much stress, and a professional cyclist's training and racing takes up a great deal of that capacity. Then there's the relationship with the team, the media, the fans, and all the rest that comes with the job. This meant Greg had virtually no energy left to deal with anything else. Everything takes a back seat to training and racing. That was a hard reality we had accepted together.

Greg was, and still is, the man I fell in love with. He made it easy for me to make sacrifices for his career. He always said that he couldn't do it without me. We were a team, and we still are. When someone really appreciates you, you love to build your life around their passion.

Greg's soigneur, Otto Jacome, was with him at

the Giro. He knew Greg was feeling bad; now Otto told him that he was looking bad, too. He said that Greg's face was actually grey, and he and the medical staff for the team convinced Greg to gave a comprehensive blood test. Those results showed that Greg was anemic. He badly needed iron.

Greg remembers: 'I had never taken an iron injection before. In fact, I hated any kind of shot so much that I would scoot around the room with my hands over my butt, trying to protect myself against the needle! The only supplement I had ever taken was a multivitamin. But I knew enough biology and physiology to realise that I had to make up for my iron deficiency. I took a shot of iron, and slowly started to feel better over the next few days.'

The cold rain which ensued eased Greg's allergies and improved his breathing. For the first time in weeks, our family was together. A snowstorm caused a cancellation of one of the stages and Greg delighted in a rare day off, playing with our little boys and being with me. Greg began to visibly relax.

'I decided to turn some of my stresses into positives,' Greg says now. 'The team wasn't paying my salary? Well, then, I guess I didn't have too much responsibility to win for them! Wives and kids were an unwelcome intrusion? Then I'd keep mine beside me for as long as I raced. I didn't have enough iron in my blood? I'd accept a shot. I began to feel so much freer, so much more like my old self.'

It was hardly surprising Greg had an iron deficiency considering he had lost so much blood during the shooting accident two years before.

Greg's mood was so improved! He gained strength each day during the rest of the Giro. By the last time trial stage, pushing himself as hard as he could, Greg finished second and was ahead of Laurent Fignon, his former team-mate and greatest rival. It was our first glimmer of hope that he was truly coming back.

Cycling analysts didn't agree. They looked at Greg's performance and figured he didn't stand a chance in the season's greatest challenge, the upcoming Tour de France. Greg and I never even dreamed he'd win the '89 Tour! We were so excited and grateful that he was regaining his physical prowess and indomitable spirit – just to make it through the Giro and onto the Tour thrilled us. Greg told me he'd be totally happy with even a 22nd-place finish.

(Can I say it? I have to say it!) And the rest is history.

Maybe all of our toughest battles are won in our hearts and minds. I don't know that, and I don't pretend to know. I do know that we remember those difficult days with near-complete clarity – maybe because they were so difficult?

At the finish of the 1989 Tour de France, with my amazing husband on the winner's podium, I was flooded with joy. Incredibly, we were back there the next year, with our three children and our parents, surrounding Greg with love. His heart and body had been terribly scarred and broken, but his mind somehow retained the ability to remain open and hopeful.

Being beside the yellow jersey after a period of bleak despair for my favourite cyclist has forever informed my feelings about this amazing sport. So I guess it really isn't surprising that I want to embrace each racer's full story; not just the bit we see out on the roads. Those stories can be pretty incredible.

Kathy LeMond married Greg LeMond in 1980, when she left university to join the pro cycling world. She spent 14 years in Europe during Greg's career and raised three children. For the past two years, Kathy has been back at races working with Eurosport.

10

During a grand tour, each rider pedals three thousand kilometres and consumes tens of thousands of calories.

Perhaps it's the frustrated restaurant critic in him, but **Lionel Birnie** has always been as interested in the food that fuels the cyclists as he has in the cuisine on offer to the travelling journalist at the Tour de France.

But he has found that, increasingly, there's more to the food on the road than meets the eye…

RAVITAILLEMENT

BY LIONEL BIRNIE

Back in 2006 or 2007, somewhere down near the Pyrenees, I was flicking through the Tour de France roadbook – the race manual given to everyone working on the race which details, among other things, the route of all the stages and the hotels the teams are staying at – when something caught my eye. The Basque Euskaltel-Euskadi team had been allocated one of those grim budget hotels on an industrial estate next to the *autoroute*, and at the bottom of the page, it said: *'Euskaltel-Euskadi. Repas: Buffalo Grill.'*

A few moments later, we passed the hotel in question and saw the team's orange vehicles crammed into the budget-sized car park, looking almost sorry for themselves. The Buffalo Grill where the riders were due to eat that evening was a short, unpleasant walk away, across a motorway bridge to an identically grim industrial state on the opposite side of the motorway.

For those who have not sampled its delights, the Buffalo Grill is a chain of restaurants, mostly based within earshot of the hum of a motorway or major road, that specialises in producing steaks that aren't as good to eat as the photographs on the laminated menu suggests they might be.

Buffalo Grill, and its immediate competitors in the chewy-meat sector – Courtepaille and the unappealingly-named Hippopotamus – aren't quite the last resort for a journalist covering the Tour de France, but it's close. The race to get to dinner before France's eccentric restaurant industry closes its doors to tired, grumpy, foreign journalists is, some years, more hotly contested than the battle for the yellow jersey. But when the clock is ticking towards 10 o'clock and the restaurants start turning off their lights and placing the chairs on the tables, it's not wise to look a gift horse in the mouth. (For legal purposes, I am obliged to point out that none of the restaurants named above serve gift horses unless the customer specifically requests one.) The only thing worse than settling for one of these grills is being forced to use a globally famous fast-food burger chain with its renowned *l'arche d'or* logo, followed closely by going hungry altogether.

For a rider taking part in the Tour, with perhaps 1,500 kilometres ticked off and another 1,500 to go, the prospect of kicking off their evening meal with a chunk of almost-frozen iceberg lettuce slathered in a blue-cheese sauce with the consistency of tooth-paste, and then following it with a steak that manages to be over-cooked and almost raw all at the same time, before concluding with half a can of squirty cream and a banana in a Knickerbocker Glory glass, eaten with a ridiculously long spoon, must surely have propelled the Euskaltel-Euskadi riders towards their breaking point.

The peloton pedals on its stomach, of course, and after a day spent eating tubes of sweet goo and energy bars that look like they are made of lovely natural stuff but have best-before dates stretching into the next millennium, the riders look forward to eating proper, recognisable food in the evening.

And so, as we continued our own race towards a soon-to-be-closed restaurant, wondering whether this might be the evening we'd stumble across a picturesque eaterie serving fine local specialties, I imagined the Euskaltel riders as they trooped across the motorway bridge, lorries thundering beneath them, and could sense their dread at what might await them. By that stage of the Tour, their team-issue tracksuits would have been hanging off their skeletal frames, bodies reduced to skin and bone because of the digestive system's constant battle to replace and process the calories burned on the bike each day.

Back then, some of the bigger teams already had a chef travelling with them at the Tour, but most did not. These days, almost all the teams at the Tour have their own chef. Either way, I would be surprised if the Euskaltel riders ate *à la carte* at the Buffalo Grill that night. It's more likely that what constituted a cyclist-friendly menu would have been laid on for them. A salad buffet of leaves, crudités and things in mayonnaise, followed by meat or fish served with a bucket of pasta in sauce. Just like the day before, and the day before that.

It's changed quite a bit in the few years since, but as recently as the mid-2000s, whenever I happened to be at a team hotel and saw the riders eating, it felt a bit like I was visiting a prison at meal time, particularly as the Tour wore on and morale sunk like heavy boots in quicksand. Meal times at the Tour still seem less like a convivial, sociable gathering of friends who chatter and laugh as they enjoy a fine meal unfolding before them and more like a chaingang, still shackled together after a hard day's toil in the blazing sun, forcing down mouthfuls of whatever is in front of them hoping it will keep them going. Perhaps that's enough of the old cyclists-as-convicts-of-the-road symbolism.

Cyclists are forced into quite a peculiar relationship with food and their weight. Food equals energy, and so they must eat a terrific amount. The old phrase about breakfasting like a king, lunching like a prince and dining like a pauper does not apply here. During the Tour, riders are constantly fuelling – after a large breakfast, they will graze on a few snacks before the start, then attempt to keep topped up throughout the race and finally, once they've finished the stage, or their warm-down, the first thing they'll be handed by their *soigneur*, or carer, is a protein shake and a little bowl of rice or pasta. But excess calories and the wrong type of foods can lead to extra, unwanted weight that they must carry around with them. Put it this way, you wouldn't choose to carry a bag of sugar up and over the Tourmalet if you didn't have to. Admittedly, during a race as long and as tough as the Tour de France, the battle is to maintain weight, stay hydrated and protect the immune system rather than worry about putting on a bit of timber and so, with the equation between power and weight so critical, the teams have, almost without exception, embraced the advice nutritionists and chefs can give about the contents and balance of the riders' diets.

Science is taking over now, which is consigning a few of the old wives' tales about food and cycling to the past. Some of those old rules seemed to verge on superstition but there is still a strand of common sense to them.

We think back to the 1960s or 1970s and assume that it was a much simpler time, and undoubtedly it was because there wasn't the information – some of it conflicting – or scientific research to read. Advice was handed down from generation to generation.

Sean Kelly's *directeur sportif* when he turned professional in 1977 was Jean De Gribaldy – a man Kelly considers to have been ahead of his time in terms of diet. De Gribaldy kept his riders hungry

– often literally. At Kelly's first training camp, he poked and prodded each rider's midriff to see if there were any podgy bits, and tutted and sucked the air through his teeth in the manner of a mechanic considering writing off a customer's car. When Kelly and his team-mates came down to breakfast on the first morning, the breakfast they were greeted with was much sparser than the hotel owner had intended. There was a small crescent-shaped grease mark on the paper tablecloth next to each plate. De Gribaldy had been down before his riders to remove the buttery croissants from temptation's way.

Even once Kelly was an established rider, De Gribaldy kept an eye on the Irishman's diet. At Paris-Nice, which often concluded with two stages on the final day – a tough road race in the morning and then the uphill time trial on the Col d'Èze in the afternoon – De Gribaldy ensured Kelly had the lightest of lunches. He would be permitted perhaps a small omelette and a tiny salad because De Gribaldy believed his rider needed to be as light as possible for the ascent of the col.

To this day, Kelly picks the soft doughy centre out of a bread roll and leaves it on his napkin because De Gribaldy told him any under-baked dough would soak up liquid and expand in his stomach, therefore slowing him down. Whether this advice stands up to scientific scrutiny is open to question but, as the Cannondale-Garmin chef Sean

Fowler told me, wheat and gluten can be irritants, especially when the digestive system is under stress, and so De Gribaldy was probably onto something.

When I first got interested in professional cycling in the 1980s, I read in books or magazines that the riders at the Tour de France had to get up at the crack of dawn so they could eat their huge breakfast three hours before the start of the stage, to give their bodies time to digest a feast that Henry VIII would have struggled to get through at such an hour.

It may have been the exception rather than the rule – a practice reserved for the longest of mountain stages, which were often six hours long, sometimes seven or even eight. But the idea of eating steak, a three-egg omelette and a bowl of pasta for breakfast, as well as cereal, fruit, bread and jam, and yoghurt, horrified me. The thought of the riders sitting down to eat these Desperate Dan-sized portions was at odds with their slender body shapes. These days during the Tour, many of the riders look so fragile you fear they might snap if they miss their footing as they step out of the team bus, but even back then they were skinny.

When Bradley Wiggins rode for Cofidis, I met him at the Four Days of Dunkirk to do a piece for a magazine on what a professional cyclist ate on a typical race day. Although it was early evening and the hotel kitchen was busy, the chef undertook the task with incredibly good grace, reproducing the

breakfast that had been laid on for the riders. There
was a bowl of porridge, a large omelette, some ham
and cheese, bread rolls with jam, quite a lot of fruit,
coffee, juice and water. One of the team's *soigneurs*
brought out the race food designed to be eaten
before and during the race – half a dozen energy
gels and bars, some 'normal' snacks such as a Mars
bar and a small can of Coke, a couple of bananas,
some small, soft rolls designed to be easy to eat on
the bike. There were two 1.5-litre bottles of water,
eight plastic *bidons* (water bottles), some with water,
some with energy drink, roughly one for every half-
hour of racing, although that would rise on a hot
day. Then there was his post-race snack, which in
this case was a ham and cheese baguette, followed by
the evening meal consisting of a large salad, a mountain of rice, some grilled chicken, a piece of fish and
some pasta, followed by fruit salad. There was also a
shake to drink before bed.

Looking at it made me feel a bit queasy, which
will surprise anyone who has witnessed me hopping
from foot to foot in anticipation upon arrival at a
restaurant that serves a really good cassoulet. But
it was the thought of eating from broadly the same
menu every day for three weeks that really depressed
me.

Part of the joy of covering the Tour as a journalist is the mixed bag of culinary delights and frights
on offer. You never know what you're going to get

because the quality of the cuisine varies as dramatically as the profile of a five-col mountain stage – from the dizzying heights of that unexpected cassoulet (a bean stew packed with duck, goose and Toulouse sausage for the uninitiated) to the plummeting lows of a leathery, gristly steak hidden under a grey sauce. When I think of Tour stages of recent years, I often associate them with the food I enjoyed or endured that day.

The fourth stage of the 2007 Tour was not particularly memorable, unless your name is Thor Hushovd, but I can still summon up the taste of the pungent cheese that concluded our meal that night. It was shaped like a volcano and dusted with red paprika, and it sat atop an impressive selection on a two-tier trolley as if it signalled the summit of the Tour's highest mountain. This king of the cheeses tasted of farmyard and was so strong I could still smell it oozing from my pores the next afternoon. Earlier on I had enjoyed an *hors-catégorie* hors-d'oeuvre of three eggs poached in beef gravy. Never had I had to chew a liquid while a colleague, Edward Pickering, opted for the escargot. Twelve snails in a special ceramic pot, each one sitting menacingly beneath the surface of some very garlicky butter. This was the culinary equivalent of riding 12 sections of *pavé* and he declared, through slightly watery eyes, eight of the snails to have been fine, although two were phlegmy, one was chewy and the other gritty.

The approach of the Pyrenees means it's nearly cassoulet time, the Alps mean melted cheese in one form or another, whether that's *raclette* or *tartiflette*. In fact, at Alpe d'Huez one year I fell foul of what I assumed had been a practical joke by the waiting staff. I ordered the *assiette de charcuterie* followed by the *raclette*. The charcuterie was a generous assortment of cold meats with cornichons and silverskin onions – so generous, in fact, that I was left looking forward to my *raclette* less than I had been. When the raclette – cheese melted in front of a flame and then scraped onto boiled potatoes in one slick move – arrived I was less than amused to see it was accompanied by the identical *assiette de charcuterie* I'd had to start with. While my colleagues chortled, I had to admit defeat. I threw down my napkin the way a defeated rider takes off his race numbers and climbed into the broomwagon.

Grumbling about sub-standard fare never goes down too well, of course, and I am aware of the dangers of fitting the journalistic stereotype of the hungry hack who has spilled the gravy train down the front of his shirt.

But on the other hand, I know only too well how a poor-quality night's sleep in some flea pit of a hotel and a terrible breakfast can get a day on the Tour off to a bad start, and so I recognise the importance of a comfortable bed and a morale-boosting meal.

Team Sky seem to have borne the brunt of

the sniggers and smirks in this regard. The idea of their staff carting nine individual mattresses around France so their riders can at least sleep on a familiar surface every night appears to be a marginal gain too far, but they are by no means the only team to do it. Their plan to use a luxury motorhome for Richie Porte at the Giro d'Italia and Chris Froome at the Tour was derided by some and barred, for the Tour, by the UCI, although surely only temporarily.

When you consider that even Team Europcar had a chef, mobile kitchen and dining car, it seems inevitable that cycling teams will seek to do every-thing they possibly can to make the unreal experi-ence of riding the Tour de France as comfortable and familiar as possible.

During the 2015 Tour, Team Sky and Ag2r spent the second rest day at a hotel next to a motorway junction. There was nothing particularly grim about that but the fact that the hotel's near neighbour was an abattoir meant the whole place was buzzing with flies.

Of course, the Tour is such a vast organisation that it swallows up hotel rooms for miles around and, over the course of the three weeks, the standard of accommodation, although variable, does seem to be evenly distributed. Each team is guaranteed its share of pleasant chateaux, although those nights are balanced out with a place that it's hard to imagine professional sportsmen would choose to stay in.

Professional cycling lags behind other sports in this respect. It's hard to imagine Premier League footballers being asked to stay in a Campanile when they travel to face Paris St Germain in the Champions League, or Formula One drivers checking into the Formula 1 just outside Monaco when the Grand Prix is on, but cyclists often have to put up with it.

Things have improved slowly, though. As recently as the late 1980s, teams were often allocated dormitories to sleep in during the Tour's mountain stages, when the pressure on hotel rooms was too great – although it is worth pointing out that the officials from ASO are never required to rough it at the budget end of the scale.

These days the team chef is as important for the morale of the riders as anything else, and as soon as there are grumbles among the riders that the menu has got a bit too familiar, the chef will move on quicker than a team leader after a winless season.

The chefs work hard to keep their menus simple, nutritious and, most importantly, varied because boredom can soon set in. And, as the Cannondale-Garmin chef Sean Fowler told me, the riders are sometimes not slow to send their feedback to the kitchen. Preparing food for the riders must be one of the toughest gigs on the Tour. Driving ahead of the riders to the next hotel, sourcing fresh ingredients from markets and supermarkets on the way and setting up their mobile kitchen; cooking for nine highly-discerning clients who are relying on those calories for their livelihood brings a certain pressure.

The working conditions vary according to team budget, too. Team Sky's kitchen and dining car is spacious enough for two chefs to work in comfort. Sean Fowler and his wife Olga work in a cramped but well-appointed Cannondale-Garmin van but still turn out food that looks like it might give the Michelin inspectors something to think about.

More important even than providing meals that are tasty and appealing, a team chef can ensure the quality of the ingredients is not compromised and know that there are no hidden fats or sugars in the food. As a grand tour unfolds, so the diet can be tailored specifically to the demands of the race, altering the balance and types of protein and carbohydrate depending on what's coming up in the race.

For a journalist covering the Tour a good meal might do wonders for morale but there's often no choice. Besides, an evening spent eating sandwiches bought from a petrol station at the wheel of the car is not going to compromise performance that much.

Lionel Birnie is the co-editor of *The Cycling Anthology*. He also presents *The Cycling Podcast* with Richard Moore and Daniel Friebe. During the 2015 Tour he made a show for *The Cycling Podcast* about food and the Tour. He writes about cycling for *The Sunday Times*. During the Tour de France, he writes Le Gourmet de France, a blog documenting his culinary journey. It can be found at lionelbirnie.com

11

Our sport is awash with cycling literature, with one of the latest examples held in your hands.

But **Samuel Abt** introduces us to one of the original and best practitioners of applying the written word to professional cycling, and a man he knew well himself: Geoffrey Nicholson

THE GREAT RACE'S GREAT BOOK

BY SAMUEL ABT

Thanks to the ascent and descent of Lance Armstrong and the boisterous opera of doping suspicions and confessions, bicycle road racing has become a fountainhead for a flood of books. Riders former and current write them (or lend their names to ghosts), *directeurs sportifs* write them, dopers write them, and even soigneurs write them – not to mention the swelling peloton of journalists with manuscripts in hand. So many books, so little time!

Once the field was uncrowded: there was a single book in English that told the reader all he wanted to know about the sport, and told him in glorious words. That book, *The Great Bike Race*, by Geoffrey Nicholson, appeared in 1977 and was an account of the Tour de France of the previous year.

Note the dates. There is no significance here – no 40th or 50th anniversary to celebrate. The main reason to talk about *The Great Bike Race* now is simply to share the pleasure of discovering a book that appears on few lists of the best writing on the sport because most of the people who compile those lists are too young to have known it.

A rare exception is the list of 50 best cycling books chosen by *Cycle Sport* magazine in 2011, which ranked *The Great Bike Race* 15th, and characterised it as 'a real historical artefact'. True enough: hardly anybody else was writing books then about the sport in English – the only other early one on the list, ranked 27th, was *Cycling Is My Life*, by Tom Simpson, published in 1966.

When he wrote his book, Geoffrey Nicholson was a 47-year-old Welshman who worked for many of the Fleet Street newspapers at one time or another as an editor, and a rugby and cycling reporter. He much preferred working in the field as a reporter to life on a desk, and devoted his later career to covering the two sports.

Before that, after national service as a lance-bombardier in the Royal Artillery (he often joked that he mainly worked as a projectionist for training films) and graduation from University College in Swansea, he worked for nearly five years in advertising. The editor Donald Trelford reported in *The Guardian* that Nicholson's high point was coining a slogan for fruit gums: 'Hey fella, Fruitella.'

Peter Corrigan said in *The Independent* that Nicholson himself was most pleased that he had noticed that a colleague's ad for Daks read, 'The trousers that stand out in front,' and had not brought this to anybody's attention before the ad ran in the papers.

Happily, he then turned full time to journalism, joining *The Observer* and, in Trelford's words, helping to transform sports reporting 'by eschewing tabloid cliches and public-relations hype and introducing a quality of writing that matched, and was sometimes superior to, that on the arts and foreign pages'.

As part of this sea change, Nicholson loved cycling for the tales it could frame.

'A race was a rounded, self-contained story with complex relationships, sudden shifts of action, identifiable heroes, a beginning, a middle and an end,' he explained early in his book. 'When it was simply a stage in a longer race, then it became another chapter in a picaresque novel which each day introduced new characters in a different setting.'

He had been to the Tour a few times when he set out in 1976 with the only other British reporters following the race – David Saunders of the *Daily Telegraph* and 'the lean and frequently hungry' Phil Liggett of *The Guardian*.

'Since I am writing only for a Sunday paper, *The Observer*, in principle I am free to spend five or six days of the week making notes for this book,' he wrote.

Those notes are gorgeous: 'One pleasure of the race is that on any day you can look out of the car window and see the makings of a photograph by Cartier-Bresson: a wedding procession walking back from the church between the banks of Tour spectators; a flock of nuns beneath a banner which says, "Poulidor, you are the strongest"; four generations of one family sitting on kitchen chairs in a doorway.'

Or: 'It is Sunday morning, when even the Swiss relax a little, and understandably there are few people on the streets.' Or: 'The Izoard is… a rocky wilderness at 7,743 feet which needs only a few bleached skulls at the roadside to complete its scene of desolation.' Or: 'The French are devoted to sport provided someone else is playing.'

Or: 'It's an area where, as the roadside notices remind us, eating and drinking aren't exactly out of favour. There is one splendid series: Foie Gras, Jambon du Pays, Confits; Confitures; Armagnac; Fruits à l'Armagnac.'

(Nicholson was renowned as a trencherman. In those days, there was a designated free lunch stop for the press – attendance voluntary – with cauldrons of dreadful hot food, sausages and cheeses, plus equally dreadful red wine; Nicholson was always to be seen near the head of the line. When departing France at the end of any of his 19 Tours, he usually stopped at a supermarket and bought a few tins of cassoulet for home consumption.)

His nuggets nestle in a book full of straightforward explanatory prose, including an inside account of how Cyrille Guimard, now a television commentator but then the *directeur sportif* of the Gitane team, forced his leader, Lucien Van Impe – six times the Tour's 'king of the mountains' – into going for overall victory grudgingly in the Pyrenees. This is all part of Nicholson's big picture.

'I thought the best way to describe the Tour was to tell, in alternate chapters, the story of a particular Tour, that of 1976,' he wrote. 'It was not one of those races dominated by a single rider: it had a series of leaders, one of whom lost control and regained it with an uncharacteristically bold attack; an elaborate web of sub-plots; the biggest stage win since the war; and a good deal more suspense than most. From that story I have moved off into the past to explain how the Tour developed its character, and its characters developed the Tour, how it is run, and how it has dealt with scandal and success.'

Nicholson was terrific at catching the essence of riders: 'Eddy Merckx, the Belgian *grand seigneur* of cycle racing, the most successful, most versatile and richest cyclist of all times, in strength of character, the noblest Roman of them all. He has the high-cheeked, graven features of a totem pole, and they break into laughter just about as often.

'Francesco Moser, a handsome downhill racer from the Dolomites who always carries with him, like a whiff of after-shave, a touch of the expensive glamour of winter sports.

'Freddy Maertens, the fastest sprinter in road racing, climbs as though he were pushing a barrel ahead of him. What Maertens asks of Flandria is simply to act as sheepdogs, keeping the flock together so that he can play the slaughterer at the finish.

'Anquetil was subtle and calculating; he used his head. Poulidor used his physical strength, forcing a confrontation in which he would gain minutes or perish. It was often the latter; a perpetual Most Unfortunate Rider's trophy might well have been struck for him.'

Sometimes, just a few words are needed: 'That banana-shaped Fernandel grin of Barry Hoban'; 'Luis Ocana, a volatile rider of undoubted class but uncertain temperament'; 'There are prizes for riders who have recently turned professional; for those who show the most combativité or who make the longest escapes. If all else fails, there are daily awards of £27.50 both for elegance and amiability which have gone to some pretty scruffy, disagreeable people.'

Nicholson is equally adept at explaining the soul of the sport: 'Road racing is a sweaty occupation. For every minute of heightened excitement and accelerating action in the sprint or the chase it demands perhaps an hour of pure drudgery, back bent under the sun, shoulders hunched against the wind and rain. The analogy with work on the land is only too obvious, and explains why so many professional cyclists, particularly in France, are recruited from the peasant smallholdings. They are used to the toil and monotony of jobs which have to be completed whatever the weather.

'The ability to ride quickly uphill is variously explained in terms of build, lightness, lung capacity, moral fibre, posture on the bike and early environment. In other words, there is no acceptable explanation.'

* * *

Is the book dated? Of course it is; Nicholson's chapters on the bicycle itself and on the riders' finances are obsolete by decades. That was the era when the race's budget, he wrote, was between £800,000 and £850,000. Contestants rode for *primes*, not green jersey points, at selected 'Hot Spots', while villages along the route offered pitifully small bonuses to the first man through – which almost everybody contested. A franc was a franc.

It was a primitive time, and Nicholson described it. 'His team car has to go ahead to the feeding station, leaving him with a folded tubular which he stuffs in his jersey pocket. If he punctures, instead of getting a new wheel in a matter of seconds, he will have to take out the wheel, strip off the old tyre, put on the new and pump it up himself, which will cost him several minutes.'

And envision this: 'Bastille Day, the longest of the Tour, though not as long as had been planned. The program of three separate stages starting at 7:20

in the morning, finishing at 6:30 in the evening and covering 362 kilometres… has [after riders' protests] been cut by 47 kilometres.'

Also obsolete are his reports on the doping problem. 'The commissaires announce that a dope test has proved positive for Jesus Manzaneque. He has been fined £230, penalised 10 minutes and will be suspended from racing for a month if he repeats the offence. It's a familiar story and a light enough sentence to ensure that we'll hear it again.'

Later: 'Bernard Labourdette, a random choice for the dope test, has been caught attempting that old trick, substituting someone else's sample of urine for his own. It's not only taken as proof of guilt, but more heavily punished than a positive analysis. He receives a fine of 5,000 Swiss francs (getting on for £1,000), demotion to last place on the stage and a 10-minute penalty on general classification.'

Nicholson never saw these penalties toughened. A jovial travelling companion and a man with uncounted friends, he died in 1999 at the age of 70 after a long battle with cancer.

His book lives on, as does he in fond memory.

Samuel Abt is the first American to be awarded the Tour de France medal for service to the race. He began writing about bicycle racing in 1977 for the *International Herald Tribune* and *New York Times* and covered the Tour 32 times. Now retired as a newspaperman, he lives in France.

The Cycling
ANTHOLOGY

If you have just discovered *The Cycling Anthology*
and have enjoyed this book, you may be
interested in the five volumes that preceded it.

Each book contains an eclectic collection of
original writing about professional cycling.

To find out more, visit cyclinganthology.com

VOLUME SEVEN
will be published in 2016.